T0279954

Everything Slows Down

My Hidden Life with Depression:
How I Survived, What I Learned

Garry Cosnett

EVERYTHING SLOWS DOWN

My Hidden Life with Depression:

How I Survived, What I Learned

GARRY COSNETT

SECANT PUBLISHING
Salisbury, Maryland

EVERYTHING SLOWS DOWN

My Hidden Life with Depression:
How I Survived, What I Learned

Copyright © 2024 by Garry Cosnett

All rights reserved. No part of this publication may be reproduced, distributed or transmitted in any form or by any means, including photocopying, recording, or other electronic or mechanical methods, without the prior written permission of the publisher or author, except in the case of brief quotations embodied in critical reviews and certain other non-commercial uses permitted by copyright law.

Secant Publishing, LLC
P.O. Box 4059
Salisbury, MD 21803

www.secantpublishing.com

Library of Congress Control Number: 2023922982

ISBN 979-8-9886410-5-6 (hardcover)
ISBN 979-8-9886410-6-3 (paperback)
ISBN 979-8-9886410-7-0 (ebook)

To my wife, Kristin, who with love changed my life story.

Contents

Author's Note

This book is a memoir of my personal experiences with clinical depression. I am not a doctor and I do not offer advice or information about diagnosis and treatment. If you have any concerns about your own health, or if you have any questions about what you read here, please seek the advice of an appropriate health professional.

The personal anecdotes recounted in this book actually happened, no matter how surreal or improbable they may seem at this remove. My hope is they may resonate with others who are suffering from depression and give hope that even at life's darkest or most humiliating points, a new beginning is always possible.

The names and identifying details of living persons who are mentioned in the pages that follow—other than public figures and the members of my own family—have been changed. Similarly, I have assigned arbitrary initials to the impressively long series of psychiatrists who have treated me. Any similarity between the fictitiously named persons and any real person of the same name is strictly coincidental.

I have chosen to pass over the story of my first marriage. That would be another book. The most important takeaway is that it gave me two children, now adults, whom I could not love more.

Introduction

One's sixty-fifth birthday is commonly a point of reflection. It certainly was for me. I was taken aback by how much of my lived experience—at least the past fifty years—had been shaped by depression. At times, it could be described as mild. And at other times, it was diagnosed as major—so severe as to be immobilizing. It was a stunning realization.

How is it that depression's role in all my life's stages was not apparent to me? I guess it's like the analogy of a fish's relationship to water. It was the medium that I lived in and moved through. At times almost invisible to me, as it was my daily companion. And at other times, so pronounced that I knew or experienced nothing else.

I write this short memoir of my life and experiences with clinical depression in the hope that it will illuminate others' path. Perhaps it will help them recognize their own struggles, and provide the reassurance of a fellow traveler. A fellow traveler who ultimately learned to manage his devastating inheritance and live a rich life, relatively depression-free.

At the same time, I hope those professionals who treat depression can find some insight here—a look into the inner experience of one suffering from chronic depression. Finally, friends and family of those depressed may find some understanding and encouragement.

Most important, this is a book about hope. Hope that even in the most pernicious cases, depression can be managed, like so many other chronic diseases. I am a living example of that possibility.

Garry Cosnett

Crash

If you drive south from Carlisle, Pennsylvania, on Route 74, past Boiling Springs, there's a two-lane bridge over the Yellow Breeches Creek. It's a high bridge and the landscape below is a deep ravine. There are lots of accidents there as it's set in an "S" curve—you can't see oncoming traffic until it approaches the midpoint of the bridge.

I set out on a snowy, late December afternoon in 1978, driving my once-beloved 1965 Ford F-100 pickup. No Christmas wreath wired to the grille that year. I was depressed. The kind of depression where everything slows down, and every move, every thought, takes effort and concentration unimaginable in a healthier state. The bridge was not my destination. But I just needed to go— somewhere. Go.

I approached the bridge with no particular plan, other than to slow down, given the snow and the blind curve. I reached for the tape deck and turned down Bob Dylan's *Blood on the Tracks* to concentrate on driving. But as I approached the mid-point of the bridge, the clearest thought I'd had in weeks jumped into my consciousness. If I speed up and swerve off the other side of the bridge, it will all be over. I jabbed the accelerator and jerked the wheel to the left.

No fear, no apprehension—a sliver of peace. But it was instantaneous. Because at that moment another pickup approached from around the blind curve. I hit him on his left-front fender and bounced back into my lane, forcing him into the left side of the bridge. Before I could even get out of my truck, the weighted blanket of depression settled in again.

Not long before this, I had learned the word for what I was experiencing, and had been experiencing, off and on for almost a decade. Growing up, my mother had "spells." And my spells didn't even have a name. To me, it was weakness, laziness, unwillingness to do what I was supposed to do. And failure to show gratitude—one of the tenets of the family "religion." It wasn't until a more sophisticated girlfriend, concerned by my seeming inability to do anything but perform my stockboy duties at B. Dalton, sleep, and watch TV with the sound turned down, diagnosed: "You're depressed." I was.

My girlfriend Cathy had taken me to community mental health, where the social worker briskly elevated my case to the attention of the medical director. Through a 20-minute interview, which I recall as very much a case of "leading the witness," the doctor concluded: "You are suffering from manic-depressive illness. We will start you right away on lithium. You will be like a newborn."

Only I wasn't. The lithium seemed to do nothing for my depression. But I lied to the doctor, saying I thought I was improving. At a point in my life where everything I did was disappointing, I didn't want to disappoint the doctor. Truth was, I was getting worse. I would head to the walk-in center at community mental health two to three times a week. Those were not productive sessions. Part of the problem was my native gift of gab and self-awareness, even at this low point. I could make myself appear, for as long as those 20-minute encounters lasted, quite a bit more OK than I truly was. Eventually, the clinic staff would just tell me to go back home and try to relax. I was the county hypochondriac.

As weeks passed, my capabilities—modest as they were—folded. Now I was spending the day on a mattress in the living room, channel-hopping in hopes of finding some message on the television that would lead me out of my state. Christmas was approaching, and the only thing it meant to me was more opportunities to disappoint.

I stopped seeing the psychiatrist, stopped the embarrassing county-subsidized purchases at the pharmacy, stopped the county health center blood-draws. Stopped the lithium.

There was one thing that gave me a sliver of relief. Driving. It got me off the mattress and into the world. And it was just that faint motivation that drove me out to Route 74 and the bridge over Yellow Breeches Creek that December day.

P.S. In recounting this frightening story to just a few of my closest friends over the years, everyone has asked the same question: "And then what?"

What happened next was almost surreal.

Neither my pickup nor the other pickup went over the side into Yellow Breeches Creek. Neither the other driver nor I were injured. It turned out neither of us wanted to call the police—me for obvious reasons; he because he was driving uninsured. The settlement we reached on the spot was that I would spend the following week digging ditches for him, and we called it even. That was the kind of work I could do well. Physical, repetitive, easy to understand. For that week, oddly enough, digging ditches brought me a kind of peace.

Spells

When my grandmother died (I was five), it wasn't difficult to imagine what death looked like. I had never seen my grandmother move—whenever we would visit, she would sit nearly motionless in an overstuffed chair, her back to the front living room window. That room may have been animated by boisterous uncles and cousins (several of whom had what I later realized to be alcohol on their breath—whatever the time of day). But grandmother, my mother's mother, sat still. A tight smile occasionally suggested approval of the room's activity. Her voice, weak and strained, always shocked when she would speak.

"Your grandmother has spells," my father would remind us as we drove home from the dreaded Sunday afternoon visits. Everything about those trips was a downer, even for a five-year-old. The unnerving silence. The startling disruption when Grandmother would actually say something. Even the setting. Bridgeton, New Jersey was a town collapsing on itself, after the big canneries (including Ritter's) deserted the county. My response when my mother told me that Grandmother had passed was, "I bet she'll like heaven a lot more than Bridgeton."

The word "spell" raised a troubling association. For Mother herself had had at least one spell I can recall by that point. She took to her bed, in a darkened room, where we three kids would be brought in once a day after Dad returned from work. The bedroom, a familiar place in our small rancher, felt strange and alienating. Mother was usually silent, or would awkwardly acknowledge us, in a striking, higher-pitched voice.

My parents, neither of whom graduated from high school, were not sophisticated people. The words "mental health" equated to craziness, as in our alcoholic uncle Kenny, in and out of institutions—and likely jail. Or Aunt Eloise, who scandalized the family by undergoing "shock therapy" in the early 1960s. Depression is not a word I ever heard spoken in the family. (Indeed, during my first hospitalization for depression, my parents told my siblings I was in "for his asthma".) Dad always had a theory on what was troubling mother: food poisoning from a "Horn and Hardart" chicken; a distracted doctor prescribing incompatible drugs. My mother's assessment was more personal and disturbing: "you kids." Alternately, it was "your father."

We always knew when a spell had taken over Mother. Without pre-announcement, her kindly and devoted brother, Uncle Dick, would meet us at the school bus stop at the end of the day. He was skilled in understatement, always reporting that "your mother is a little under the weather and needs her rest." So for days, sometimes a couple of weeks, Uncle Dick would prepare our meals, oversee our homework (to the best of his sixth-grade abilities), and serve as our liaison with the sequestered mother. Every few days, Dad would take us into the bedroom, where our mother would be alternately silent, or blaming (chicken, Dad, us).

Spells would end, seemingly, as unexpectedly as they began. One morning, at breakfast, Uncle Dick would have his bag packed and ready to go to the bus station. Mother would emerge, frail and unsteady, and without a word of what had just transpired. We had learned not to say a word, either. Pretending it never happened became the family's unique expertise.

Over time, the spells became more frequent, lasted longer (always weeks now), and seemed to never fully lose their influence over Mother. Even in her healthier periods, she was pessimistic and obsessed with safety—or should I say, danger. It was everywhere. My then-teenage sister got the worst of her fantastic anticipation of things that could go terribly wrong—after all, she was out in the world. My fraternal twin Gilbert and I received constant lectures on whatever her latest phobic obsession happened to be (we could anticipate some of them by glancing at the contents of the current *Readers' Digest*).

And the spells: they now were driven, in my mother's self-diagnosis, by where we lived. The neighbors; the schools; the climate; the state. We moved seven times— in three states—by the time I was in seventh grade. Each time there would be, at first, a sense of collective relief. But then, a spell would reemerge, and we would need to move again. My father was baffled, and no doubt angry, but move we would. To California; back to New Jersey; to Florida; back to New Jersey. The spells, of course, followed close behind.

Family Sketches

G iven the frequency, depth, and disorientation of my mother's spells, each family member responded to them, and was ultimately shaped by them, in markedly individual ways.

I'll take a look at each, but understanding the context requires a snapshot of the family ethos. Kindness was the foundation of each of our personalities. Overlooking the relatively harsh hand dealt my parents—leaving school in high school to bring money into the family; working unsatisfying jobs just to get by; living at the bottom of the social order in a wealthy Philly suburb—they generally cultivated an attitude of appreciation. And always, kindness.

As my therapist Blanche observed in her Alabama lilt: "Your parents were dear sweet people, Garry, but they never taught you there are TIGERS out there!" She was right. Fraternal twin brother Gilbert, and big sister Joyce (and I), moved out into the world with the expectation of good character in (most of) the people we met. It was frequently a disadvantage.

A second characteristic that shaped all of us was intimidation—deference, actually—regarding the professional class. As my mother once said after a psychiatric session, when we asked what the doctor said about her recurring nightmares: "I don't talk about things like that, he'll think I'm crazy."

Finally, and related, was a strong sense of class consciousness. Not a brand based in bitterness, but a clear sense that you know your place and your bond to people at the same station. Gilbert violated this precept when he bought a house in "the rich section." My mother blamed one of her spells on that simple, yet profound, effort at self-betterment. "We don't belong over there with the doctors and the lawyers."

Mother

Born in 1918, youngest of eleven in a family of nearly classical dysfunction. Alcoholism, philandering, gambling debts, and lack of interest in the family—that was her father. Many of these traits trickled down to the boys of the family. And at the center, depression. My grandmother's depression was the clearest, most obvious. But as I've moved through my own depressions, I am more confident that there were multiple depressions in that family—just different brands of self-treatment.

My mother, Sara (Sally), seemed determined to break out of that unfulfilling (to say the least) world. Quit school, got a relatively well-paying job. Would take the bus to Atlantic City for dances in the Steel Pier ballroom. Always naturally pretty and petite, she was known as quite the dresser. Would catch another bus to Camden to shop at "Ray's," whose motto was "Dress Today and Pay Ray Payday." She did, many times.

That Sally, as far as I know, sought a better life, with a little adventure thrown in. She dated my father—popular with the girls—who owned a motorcycle, and a share of an airplane! Soon after they were married, Dad asked my grandmother's permission to move his bride to Florida. "Yes. Go. Take her away from here, Gil." Sobs followed.

If they were going to do this, they were going to *really* do this. Off they went to Miami in the 1940s. Dad would rent a seaplane and Mother would pack a picnic to enjoy right in the middle of Biscayne Bay. Dad landed a flight mechanic job for Eastern Airlines, and mother worked the counter at the exclusive Burdines Department Store. Photographs from that time reveal the energy and promise they were cultivating.

When did the spells begin? I never learned. If I may speculate, the first was when she lost a child at delivery, the cord wrapped around his neck. My understanding is that they just didn't talk about it afterward, on the advice of the family physician. But certainly the spells had begun by the time the twins were born, five years later.

We would see glimpses of "Miami Mother" throughout her life. She was known among my high school friends for her more-than-passable Elvis impersonation (*Heartbreak Hotel* was her signature number). I, in particular, was her pride and joy—a role that both brought me joy and confusion. But during the spells there was no music. The sound system I installed in her kitchen was silent, or worse, so low as to be just audible. There was something creepy about that.

I won't go through all her hospitalizations and treatments. I honestly lost track; we all did. After we had exhausted the family's resources, our only option was the county hospital. It was as dreadful as one might imagine. But the enlightened University of Pennsylvania psychiatrist she saw, working pro bono, prescribed electroconvulsive therapy (ECT)—known in the past as "shock treatment," followed by lithium and nortriptyline. That course of treatment changed our lives. Mother lived seven years relatively depression-free. It wasn't until Alzheimer's set in that we saw her revert to a condition as bad as her worst spell, and then beyond, deeper.

I want to come back to my first observation about my family. Mother was, when well, a deeply caring person—probably too empathetic for her own good. But I do remember so many kind moments growing up, and beyond. It always made the transformation all the more stunning when she entered her angry and blaming mode that characterized the spells.

Dad

No doubt, my father was the most complex "simple man" I ever knew. Born in 1910, and turning nineteen at the dawn of the Depression, he became an itinerant water tower painter, using a rig he designed and built. In later years, he labored as a machinist, but had an engineer's intelligence and an inventor's creativity. He was a surprisingly good writer as well. One of the most moving experiences of my life was when I went from shop to shop where he worked, to deliver the news that Gil had died. I heard amazing stories of his innovations and craftsmanship. Sadly, he found it hard to feel rewarded by his work, always intimidated by those more educated.

The stories were moving, but more so was the frequent observation "your father was an 'ace.'" That he was. His lessons in kindness stayed with me a lifetime. And honesty. Oh boy, you had better be truthful. His common expression: "I can't stand a bull-crapper; a bull-crapper is not worth a goddamn," was delivered with no sliver of equivocation. (It may have been inspired by his older brother, who was a bull-crapper of the first order.)

It was Dad who took the brunt of Mother's spells. Either he was being blamed for them, or he was the one stuck with doing all the legwork for the self-prescribed therapy that involved getting out of Dodge and starting over in another state. I never witnessed his spirit broken, but it must have been—in private. He relied on Mother's brother, Uncle Dick, to help with the kids when Mother was immobilized. He often worked two jobs, but would try to be home for supper in between. I really understood "tired" by simply watching his face as he left the table to report to Job #2. He worked past his eightieth birthday, within just a few weeks of his death.

Occasionally, he would express his frustration to me, confiding that he could not have a normal marriage. And that "your mother won't let me do what I want to do"—in one memorable case, resuming skydiving. No doubt foreseeing the worst, she put her foot down.

Still, Dad stayed sharp and devoted to Mother until his sudden death from acute leukemia. That was a trigger for Mother's worst spell ever.

Big Sister Joyce

Joyce fit right into the family ethos, and then some. I may be straining my credibility here, but a kinder person I have not met. Joyce was a big influence on her twin brothers, especially in her high school years when she introduced us to the world of British rock/pop. She took us out in her '57 Chevy and bought us our first 45 rpm records. I find that memory just as clear as a movie scene, fifty-five years later. And she was *fun*. She was our ambassador to 1960s pop culture, and I still smell "Aqua Net" hairspray when I hear The Zombies or The Animals on satellite radio.

The spells shaped all of us, and perhaps Joyce most of all. She was the one Mother called on for assistance in her later years. Some of those encounters must have been downright scary. Mother could seem nearly possessed by another spirit when she was at her worst.

Joyce built a kind of bubble around herself—"Joyceland," as her adult daughters, my nieces, have labeled it. I guess it was her way of coping with all the chaos we grew up with—especially the uncertainty and seeming randomness of affection from my mother. Anxiety was Joyce's issue, perhaps a direct reaction to the life our family led. Or, perhaps, part of the family's biological inheritance. Joyce has not ventured far from our hometown and prefers the familiar in everything—including recently reuniting with her high school boyfriend in a reprise of the Sixties. "Joyceland" is generally adaptive, and works, but recently, post-retirement, depressions have set in. It has to be scary. But it has brought the two of us closer together as I can share my own dark experiences and, ultimately, successes, in battling our shared legacy.

Fraternal Twin Gil

Gil is an enigma—not the most original sentence, but expressive nonetheless. He was a kid of many borderline obsessions, including exploring the Midwestern states which he never had visited. He had thick files of town brochures, newspapers, and replies to the countless letters he dispatched beginning with, "My family and I are considering a move to Creston, Iowa" —or Wooster, Ohio, or dozens of other more or less randomly selected localities in the nation's heartland.

This obsession even pervaded his sleep: he would visit an imaginary town at a particular part of his dream cycle, set his alarm clock for that time, wake up and take notes and sketches. He was certain he would find that town sometime, and he wanted evidence he had dreamed it.

I remember coming home from a dance one night during high school. Gil handed me the receiver of the yellow Western Electric wall phone. "That phone is ringing in Creston, Iowa—is that amazing?" I was less than amazed. But I now believe the rich fantasy life Gil developed was his way of insulating himself and wresting some sense of control over a life in which our family frequently, and with little warning, went off the rails.

Sometimes this need to control was directed toward me. He ended my brief songwriting career in seventh grade when he pronounced my social protest song,

"Plastic People of Society," to be "really stupid, Gar." I never made another attempt.

Gil went on to be a paramedic, and had the opportunity to work in nuclear safety, right after the Chernobyl disaster. Never squeamish, he lectures broadly on the effects of radiation as a highly regarded nuclear safety consultant. He handles a demanding role with aplomb and a seeming absence of anxiety. And I've never detected signs of depression in Gilbert. He's the family outlier.

I Didn't Have
a Word for This

"That truck is going to hit the building!" I was transfixed by the spectacle of a semi, backing treacherously close to the buff brick wall of Camden County College. I watched, rapt, for several minutes, until the driver finally hit his target—the loading dock. A few minutes wasted. Except I was in the middle of my SAT, math section. And I couldn't concentrate.

The concentration issue had actually begun several months earlier. It was my junior year, and I was able to maintain my strong grades, but the effort it required seemed to grow like compound interest. I applied for, and received, a rarely bestowed privilege: Independent Study status. This allowed the student—me—to flash a card at the main office, sign myself out, and head to Philadelphia to research a major project. Mine was to answer the question: "Can photography be fine art?" I still had to meet the requirements of my regular classes, but was able to escape when my concentration was so bad that being in class was of no value.

I'm not sure if I applied for the program to accommodate my state of mind, which in retrospect, was depressed. Or whether I was truly driven to answer that research question. The configuration, compelling on the surface, proved dangerous to someone who was experiencing a major depression.

I would sign myself out, take the train into Philly, and go to one of the major university libraries—particularly the fine arts library at the University of Pennsylvania. It was in a famous late 19th century church-like building by the revered Philadelphia architect, Frank Furness. Just sitting there, originally, lifted my mood. I was a real scholar. Except I wasn't. My concentration "issue" made it progressively difficult to do fundamental research. I would read Walt Whitman to distract myself. Over time, the Furness Library took on a creepy air, and I stopped going. The Philadelphia public library was a more forgiving space, given its unapologetic blandness.

The master plan of the Independent Study was to do my primary research in the spring semester, then write my thesis over the summer. As summer approached, I panicked. I had a notebook of short bursts on photography, questions about my mental state, reflections on "society," and coded wishes to no longer exist.

It wasn't long before I recognized that I just could not do the thesis. Even if I started my research in earnest in June, I lacked the mental focus and energy to do what I hadn't been able to do in the spring. Further, the whole idea of art photography began to sicken me. I sold my once-beloved 1950s Nikon rangefinder camera. And I knew I had to tell the school that I'd failed the project.

I made an appointment with the principal, Mr. Watson. One sweaty early July afternoon I walked down to the high school, in my (only) tie, to confess my sins.

I told Mr. Watson that I was devastated by a breakup with my girlfriend, and that I found myself unable to concentrate or do the thought work on my project. There were probably two lies here: I was actually quite relieved by the breakup, which I had initiated. And, somehow, I was able to perform well on my "regular" schoolwork (with some guidance from my MIT-bound best friend Phil). Mr. Watson was surprisingly okay with the aborted independent study project (this was the mid-'70s, and "relating" was the dominant model of administrative behavior). But he was concerned about my mental health and encouraged me to "get some help" processing my breakup. I honestly didn't see how getting some "help" would actually help. I attributed my failure to some endemic laziness or lack of character. If I were mentally ill, help might help. But I was simply deficient.

My relief was short lived when I realized my last chance to take the SAT was fast approaching. I bought one of the state-of-the-art study guides and went straight to the practice tests. I did not do well, which surprised me, and it sent me back to the preliminary material. Concentration failed me again, and I took on a "what will be will be" attitude. Besides, at that point, I couldn't imagine starting college, especially a "good" one, as this was what my competitive classmates were clamoring for.

Which brings me to the test at the community college. I was out drinking the night before. Drinking would give me an excuse if I didn't do well. And, as I had discovered earlier that summer, it quieted my anxiety over my mental state. Beer was my anti-anxiety med, but it wasn't clear to me that it was further deteriorating my mood.

I took a job delivering laundry for a local dry cleaner but consistently screwed up the orders. I was afraid of getting fired, so I quit as a preemptive strike to cut lawns.

That I could do, though I had a mindless encounter with an electric hedge trimmer.

I spent the rest of the summer cutting grass, drinking beer, and working on my $450 van. While my friends were on college tours to the Middleburys, Colgates, and Oberlins of the world, I scheduled an "interview" at Camden County College. They looked at my scores and offered me a special program, noting that a recent grad from my town had transferred to Brown. That was not enticing—it was scary.

In September, school resumed—my senior year. Mood was still down. Concentration issues merged with sleep problems. I couldn't get to sleep at night; couldn't get out of bed in the morning.

The first week back in school, I was called to the guidance office. "Crap," I thought—they want to nail me for the Independent Study project. I was wrong. Mr. Wells informed me, with brightness in his voice (and a touch of incredulity), "Your SAT scores are quite strong. Let's get you into college." I had no enthusiasm for the prospect. Even the community college seemed like too much. Lawns always need cutting. Maybe I could add snow removal.

Going East

I skipped school one afternoon my junior year to see the movie *Siddhartha*. I had read the Hermann Hesse novel a year earlier (while depressed—it was a struggle), and I thought the film version would be easier on my limited powers of concentration. There was no immediate revelation from either the book or the film, but a seed took root: Perhaps "going east" was my route out of depression.

I loaded up on Ravi Shankar cassettes and attempted to transcend my blue mood with what you could crudely call meditation (I had no idea what I was doing, but there was much *Om*-ing).

A friend convinced me that what was missing was a psychedelic experience—it was a shortcut to enlightenment. I had given up on pot—if I smoked twice a week, I would be practically nihilistic by Saturday. Eastern tranquility this was not. But he assured me this was different. "Acid is about tranquility—and seeing through illusions." Very Siddhartha-like, I thought.

Three of us planned to trip on a weekend when one set of parents was on their annual church canoe trip in the Jersey pines. Perfect. We "dropped" mid-morning, and found ourselves lying in the elementary schoolyard, watching the sky. Perhaps inspired by my imaginary girlfriend, Joni Mitchell, I saw an airliner sweep across the field, then turn at a 120-degree angle as it became a gliding hawk.

We retreated to Glen's house where we put on Pink Floyd and Emerson, Lake, and Palmer (the other guys were decidedly not interested in my Ravi Shankar contribution). We were watching the furniture in the living room breathe in time with the music, and engaging each other in very heavy conversation about, well, REALITY.

Soon reality bit. Up the driveway came a very elongated Ford Country Squire, puffing like the *Soul Train* locomotive, with what looked like two 30-foot and very bendy canoes on top. It was pouring rain—a fact we had missed in our consideration of reality—and the canoe trip was bagged.

Holy shit. We needed a story fast: "Ok, this is what we'll say: We tried pot for the first time—and we hate it!" Glen's parents told us to go outside and brush the dirt and leaves off our jackets (from the schoolyard). I brushed the back of Glen's jacket, and the embroidered eagle jumped off and flew away. Man, this would be hard to pull off.

Going back inside, Glen decided to take the floor and explain:

"We were on a swing and it was going around and then it was going up and down and we were on a swing..." HE WAS BLOWING IT. "What is wrong with your eyes, boys?" Mrs. Wilson kept asking.

I took the floor. "Well, you see, Mrs. Wilson, we tried marijuana, and it made us really sick feeling, and the bird flew off Glen's jacket." There, that would explain it...

Mrs. Wilson said, "I'm calling each of your mothers, right away. But I don't know you" (pointing to me). I bolted and ran. Fortunately, neither of the other guys revealed my identity. I took off for Main Street and stuck out my thumb. Some jock-type kids in a convertible picked me up, put me in the back seat, and proceeded to play games with my head. I begged them to let me out and they finally did—in the woods.

The trees had gargoyles—squirrel-like. But bigger, with glistening teeth. The sticks on the ground formed arrows on the purple sand, directing me. Finally I came to a clearing and a phone booth. I would call one of my druggie friends to help me. And I had a quarter! Frustratingly, the numbers on the dial kept jumping. Then the dialer started to spin itself. I did get my quarter back. But it was no good to me.

It was still raining off and on (I think) and I was soaked. Going home was my only realistic option at that point. And I was coming down from the LSD. I walked into 20 Colonial Avenue (purchase price $11,900) and proceeded to trip over the first step to the upstairs. My parents were in the middle room, watching *All in the Family*, and asked me to come in and say hello. I said I was sick. I made it upstairs to the bathroom, then the five more steps to my room. Where my posters were having an all-out war. Jimi Hendrix was prevailing, with sharp little darts flying from his Fender.

A knock on the door, and the door opened, revealing my mother and her cure-all, Pepto-Bismol! This was problematic, first because I was fascinated by its glistening and perfect pinkness on the spoon. "Well, take it…" Problem number two was the spoon was bending and drooping and stretching and impossible to catch. I closed my eyes and opened my mouth, and Mother landed the plane as she might have done when I was a toddler.

Finally home, I methodically removed my wet clothes, watched the posters settle into a cease-fire, and turned on my home-made stereo with the ridiculous ottoman-sized speakers. And what would be starting on the underground station, WMMR? Buzzy Linhart's *The Love's Still Growing.* A trippy, eastern-drone inspired raga-ballad. I was tranquil, and drifted off to sleep.

The overall experience deepened my depression and convinced me I had damaged my brain. Yet I was still hoping that turning East would be my answer. In subsequent years I tried vegetarianism (six years, no effect on mood); serious yoga (four years, no effect on mood); and joined a meditation group. This final stage was promising, except for the overt competitiveness of those collected to pursue enlightenment. After each meditation, there was considerable one-omsmanship as each meditator tried to top the others' recounting of their experience. Mood was affected negatively.

I finally concluded that if I were going to overcome my chronic depression, I would have to do so as a working-class kid from the wrong side of the tracks in the right town in New Jersey. Not very "Eastern." In fact, to finish off this saga, I once dated a very rich girl whose father, a doctor, had made his fortune with some medical device. She, however, was totally immersed in things Eastern, and announced our relationship would never work because I was "so Western." She was probably right.

Senior Year:
Mood Experimentation

S o far, nothing I tried to emerge from my dark place was working—at least not for very long. Entering my senior year, I was determined to transcend the painful state I had been living in for the past six months. I knew I could mow lawns, but now I was back in school. And Mr. Wells was calling me in weekly to plan for college.

He asked me what colleges I visited over the summer. I said "none," as the county college did not count as a "real" college in my ultra-competitive high school. The Ivies were the state religion, as the window stickers on every Volvo and Mercedes station wagon would testify.

"Have you EVER visited a college?"

"Well yeah, I took a Presbyterian group college tour last year. They were all a blur when I got back. Except..."

"Except?"

"The College of Wooster," in Ohio. I thought that place seemed pretty nice. And they had an impressive campus radio station. Maybe I could do something with that.

I had actually taken the college tour to spend five days with my Presbyterian girlfriend. I had no interest in—or expectations concerning—colleges. But I even got a "scholarship" to take the tour (we were decidedly working-class in a decidedly upper-class town). Off we went on the luxury motorcoach for two colleges a day, ten total. A blur, mostly. But the formal "tea" at Bucknell made me very sure of what I did not want.

Mr. Wells asked his secretary to connect him with the admissions office at The College of Wooster. I was freaking—it was too tangible and too fast. But he made a pitch for me with me sitting there—it honestly sounded like he was talking about someone else. But by the end of the phone call, he congratulated me. I was going to college. Somewhere in Ohio.

At least now I had something to say when the conversations turned to colleges. It wasn't Amherst, but some people had heard of it. I was in the game.

I had no idea if I'd ever find my way to Wooster, Ohio. But my acceptance did give me cover. And it was very helpful in dating, where the fathers' first two questions were "what street do you live on?" (big fail here), and "where are you going to college?" (passing grade). And the timing was more than fortunate, as I thought I could use dating as a way out of my funk.

Dating I could somehow pull off, at least initially. I was someone new, even though I'd been around for three years, focused mainly on my rock band and conspicuous alienation. What I needed to do was to date the right kind of girl, and I would be catapulted out of my distressed state. Actually, the depression was lifting at this point, slowly, organically. I had a little momentum going into my experiment with different kinds of friends (not just rockers)—and girlfriends.

Not sure how I pulled it off, but I dated a sporty girl, a popular girl, an arty girl, and, quite briefly, a druggie girl. Finally found brainy girls to be the best match. The problem was, these relationships weren't durable. Not just because it was high school. Once they got to see my darker side, their enthusiasm dropped precipitously ("this is supposed to be fun"). And, once I saw that each relationship was not the key to unlock my dark moods, my enthusiasm dropped as well.

All through this experiential-experimental phase, college edged closer. That summer I relied heavily on my beer therapy (the drinking age in New Jersey was then 18), concluded that marijuana made everything worse, cut lawns, and painted houses. I was making what seemed like pretty good money. And I knew I could do these jobs without screwing up. So I announced to my parents that I didn't need college—I was going to be a professional handyman.

This message was received with mixed reactions: on the one hand, there was deep disappointment. I would have been the first in the family to attend college (my older sister was the first to graduate from high school). On the other hand, there was always subtle pressure not to leave the family, leave the social class—not to turn into a "better." So becoming a handyman was in a deep and probably unhealthy way, a sign of allegiance to the family.

Only, I discovered being a handyman could bring on a blue mood as well. After I finished painting (four colors!) a lovely Victorian cottage (and dating the talented girl they hired to reglaze the ornate windows), I was engaged by Mrs. Cadillac to replace the chains in her hundred-year-old double-hung windows—three floors' worth. It was the dirtiest job I'd ever taken on—one hundred years of dust, grime, and pollen disturbed by every move of my prybar. All the while Mrs. Cadillac was watching and providing running commentary on my efforts, while joylessly quoting the Old Testament Book of Ecclesiastes— "All is vanity," and other uplifting verses.

My next assignment was clearing a building lot. That required a chainsaw and all the landscaping tools I had in my van. So elemental. Until the end of the ten-hour day, when I discovered poison ivy covering every last inch of exposed skin (I was hoping for a manly tan). Next, landscaping at a local fiberglass factory, with pink dust flying.

"I can't do this forever." My mood was dropping again—no matter what I tried. I sent a $100 admission acceptance check to the College of Wooster.

College, Part 1

The first correspondence I got from Wooster was my acceptance letter (no dramatic surprise here), some standard forms, and a roommate questionnaire. I definitely did not want a roommate, so I figured I'd game the system. I put together the strangest and most inconsistent profile that my imagination would accommodate. It was a calculated bet: I would either get a single, or be matched with a total nut job. My calculation paid off when I was notified that I would occupy a single in the top floor of Kenarden Lodge. I looked it up in the college "viewbook"—it reminded me of the Furness Library at Penn. Maybe I could be a real scholar this time. At the same time, a single room was probably not the best configuration for someone who suffered from "spells."

My brother drove me to Wooster. I think my parents' ambivalence discouraged them from the classic family ritual. He brought his girlfriend, Leslie, along, and we spent a night at a discount hotel, drinking bad beer (3.2%). The conversation was driven by both Gilbert's and Leslie's assertions that they were not going to do college. The deeper we got into the evening, the more my impulse to return to Jersey with them grew. Yet I knew I couldn't fail again, and the next morning I was ready to make my home in Kenarden Lodge.

How was my mood at this juncture? Anxious, for sure. But the dark feelings had lifted again, and I sensed the possibility of living with relative emotional comfort. College was a revelation: so many fields to immerse myself in. Motivated colleagues. Learning for learning's sake.

As is the beginning of so many college stories, I met a young woman during orientation week. She was a bit hippie-ish, but had come from boarding school. A compelling combination: I had known some preppies in my hometown, but Mills (short for Millicent) was softer, kinder. And was not terribly interested in beer or drugs—I could get healthy!

That we came from different worlds was progressively clear. Her family had several homes. And live-in "help." And were more-or-less full-time philanthropists. I learned most of these unsettling characteristics from a couple of drunk guys from her hometown. I was afraid that I couldn't keep up, and that premonition proved to be more than reflexive paranoia.

About halfway through the fall semester my mood was slipping. Concentration was becoming more difficult, getting to my morning classes more of an ordeal. Procrastination was setting in. And it was showing up in my grades.

I went to see the dean of students, hoping he could offer some advice about managing my low mood. But by that time I had come to blame the college for my distress, and ended up in a debate with him about the conservative bias of many of the school's policies. He suggested that they were not likely to change. He was actually good-natured about it. Further, he reasoned that I could get a great education there if I learned to overlook some of my frustrations. That seemed both compelling and impossible.

Mills and I had broken up for the first time, and I was borderline immobilized. The timing was abysmal: heading into finals. My biggest source of anxiety was not the legendary four-hour final in "European Architecture in the Classical Tradition, 1400-1800." It was the final speech in "Communication 101: Persuasive Speaking." I could not get it together to write that speech, a speech that would be given to the entire communication department. The speeches ran for three days, and mine was on day one (Monday). After a weekend of worry, avoidance, and escape fantasies, I had basically nothing. I planned to catch the professor first thing and lobby to reschedule my speech. But it was like talking to a brick wall. "No way—the schedule is set. You WILL speak at 10:00 this morning."

I ran back to my room—it was now 8:30—and grabbed a book I was reading for a sociology course, *The Pursuit of Loneliness*. I would speak on alienation, and with intentional irony, would argue that the "audience" was structurally alienated from the "presenter." This was not a theme in the book, but I thought it suited the occasion. I placed bookmarks carefully in the several pages that I planned to quote from. It was now 9:50—just enough time to run to the speech building. Through the oak grove...

I tripped. A gnarly root of one of the revered oaks did me in. My ankle was twisted. Worse, my book flew from my hand, dropping bookmarks like leaves. I was in trouble.

It was not just my self-critical impulse that led me to conclude the speech was a disaster. Everyone was given a one-page evaluation sheet from his or her individual professor. Mine was attenuated. "This is a speech?" was the entire text, scratched boldly through a quarter of the page.

My mood tested new lows. The one blessing in this fiasco was that this was my last final. I had done reasonably well in the others (I can usually muster an hour or so of clarity unless I'm at my lowest.) This capability would become a liability when I first sought mental health treatment. I presented myself as more well than I actually was.

Winter break: I struggled with the question of whether to return to Wooster or take advantage of the excessively snowy winter, buy a snowplow for my truck, and return to the handyman existence.

College, Part 2

J ust as my mother blamed the neighborhood (or the actual house) for her depression, I blamed colleges. I would apply, enroll, find I was still depressed—or more depressed—and drop out.

Consider these examples:

The College of Wooster

I dropped out twice, having re-entered my sophomore year. I found a volunteer position in an off-campus program house, "Meyers Drop-In and Referral Center." I was a peer counselor. The problem with that was the problems of students I counseled seemed small compared to my perpetual blue mood. I was ineffectual. Academically, I had changed my major for the third time, to Philosophy. Mistake. Now I had the puzzles of existence itself to ruminate on. I declared a minor in Art—I thought if I were going to wrestle with the nature of reality, I could at least work it out in tangible form. I did poorly in philosophy; I did very well in art.

Tyler School of Art

I transferred as a conditional student to Temple University's art school. I really thought this would be the fix for my depression—what credible artist isn't a little mentally ill? I built non-functional jewelry. Well, technically functional, but too heavy or awkward to actually wear. I guess it was my statement of sorts. The head of the metals department thought my designs were terrific and wanted me to stay full time. But I was drifting deeper into depression, and getting myself to the studio was becoming a daily ordeal. The "fix" this was not.

University of Pennsylvania night school

Again I placed my hope in a college. This time I thought I could combine philosophy and art in the study of art history. And what a place to do it. I found myself back in the Furness Art Library, this time really feeling like I belonged there (well, as much as a night student could). Some of the classes were quite good, taught by regular day faculty. But two were awful, taught by graduate students whose idea of erudition was obfuscation. I could not follow their lectures, and the readings were nearly as arcane. On the last day of drop-add, I dropped all my courses and headed to Maine to play music and build a house (a geodesic dome!) with a friend.

Earlham College

When the Maine thing didn't work out (there turned out to be hunters all over the property, despite the copious signs), I thought I'd apply to a more hippie-ish college. I had been attending a Friends Meeting, and expected enthusiasm when I announced I was off to a Quaker college. "Don't burn thyself," was the response of a vocal member of the congregation. I came to understand her meaning in time. Earlham, while Quaker to the core, was still a small liberal arts college with all the issues and drama that goes along with them. I became disillusioned pretty quickly—or maybe I was projecting my depression onto the school. But by the second semester, I dropped all my academic courses and focused on art. And began my transition to townie.

Stockton State College/ Richard Stockton College of New Jersey/Stockton University

Stockton started out in 1968 as New Jersey's Experimental College. No grades; no majors (only "concentrations"); no sports; and in many classrooms, no desks or chairs (carpeted pods). The evolution of the name reflects the evolution—or devolution—of the college, as it became more and more mainstream. But it was always my go-to between other colleges. They were always happy to take me back—the prodigal student. I became good friends with several faculty who had joined when the college started in the old Mayflower Hotel on the Atlantic City boardwalk. "Mayflower pilgrims," as they are known. I got a great education at Stockton. It was a place where I was so comfortable that I could still do okay even when feeling down. The profs were understanding and accepting—I think depression was the family disease they shared.

I did some significant independent research on the symbolism of residential architecture. And fell in love with, of all things, philosophy of science. My philosophy professor encouraged me to apply as a special student to Princeton, to do advanced coursework in that area. The process was arduous, but I gained acceptance—just as I was getting that slowing sensation again. I panicked, feeling I wasn't up to it, and cancelled my registration. This failure still stings.

I did, however, graduate from Stockton at age 26. With honors in social and behavioral sciences (my concentration).

University of Iowa—Graduate School

Based on my Stockton work, and the other pieces of my educational montage, I applied, and was accepted to the Ph.D. program in American studies at Iowa. Further, I was offered the top humanities fellowship in the University—five years all tuition paid, plus a stipend. I moved to Iowa City that summer to take summer courses in my weak area: history. Depression had been building since my Stockton graduation, and it really took over that summer. I struggled mightily to get all A's—anything less would look bad re: my fellowship. I pulled it off, but at the cost of exhaustion. When the fall semester began, I met my entering classmates. One had a piece in the current *Atlantic*, another had recently published a book. They all seemed so much more accomplished than me. And certainly more confident. My fellowship must have been a mistake.

I approached my advisor, and he asked how much I thought I could do. Maybe I could keep the fellowship with one semester of part-time study. I replied that I didn't think I could do anything. He was clearly angry. I thought they would just pass my fellowship to the next in line, but no, he explained, the department would lose it. I signed away my fellowship that afternoon and dropped all my classes. I would run into my advisor from time to time in town, and he would greet me, quite unsympathetically.

Iowa, Take Two

I didn't want to return home in defeat, so I took a job as a shipping clerk at The University of Iowa Press. It was probably at the outer reaches of my capabilities at that point. I did, though, find it satisfying. Sending books all over the world. Sometimes to famous authors, like William Styron (author of depression memoir *Darkness Visible*—ironic). As a university employee, I could take up to two courses per term, tuition free. So I took a graduate communication course, then another, then a third. I got to know the professor, and confessed my American studies mishap to her. She encouraged me to apply to the communication studies program, and reassured me that she would give me cover when or if I found myself depressed again.

I applied, was accepted, and began the Ph.D. program. I did have a hospitalization for depression in my third year (#2), but Stacey was good to her word, found someone to cover the courses I was teaching, and gave me a break on assignments. I took my comprehensive exams at the end of the year, got honors and a pro-forma MA degree. I realized the academic life was not for me, and I left the program, albeit this time with a significant credential.

Hospital, Part 1

I had just dropped out of college #4, Earlham, a small Quaker college in Richmond, Indiana. Certain that its scale (human), values (Quaker), and geography (small city in the Midwest) would be the antidote to the then-depressing University of Pennsylvania, I had matriculated at Earlham, age 23.

How could it be that after a few weeks of Quaker engagement, depression settled in—just as it had in colleges #1 – #3? I started dropping classes until I had only photography and ceramics remaining on my schedule. I couldn't keep my financial aid with a part-time course load, so I started a job search. Ironically, I found one at the local Community Mental Health Center: Dunn CMHC—five-county catchment area (all the way up to Muncie!). I was the new "statistical clerk." I calculated the ratio of schizophrenic admissions in one county vs. the other four; could tell you how many OCD cases were treated in Franklin County, and how this compared with neighboring Wayne.

I screwed up the numbers—a lot. I struggled to concentrate. But I was determined to get them right. I asked for more hours and was—despite my performance issues—promoted to three-quarter time. That was enough to live on as a "townie." I moved into a $165/ month apartment over *Weight Watchers* downtown. Sold my VW bus. Bought an old Chevy Nova—metallic green with countless rust accents. Even found a townie girl-friend who had never been to college! This was *me*. This was my answer.

The irony deepened when my depression intensified. One Friday evening, after wrestling with my numbers at work for seven hours, I sunk into the deepest depression I had experienced yet. I was desperate. I grabbed a bottle of J&B scotch by the throat and tried to down it. Couldn't even do that. Terrified, I slouched to the corner of my bedroom and called—inevitably—Dunn Community Mental Health. By that point, I was having, for the first time, hallucinations. I could not tell where the far wall in my room ended. I would look up at the ceiling, try to follow the crown molding to the corner, but it would just blur out as I approached the corner.

A social worker that I worked with answered the crisis line, and I described my state. She encouraged me to drive (!) to the emergency room of the community hospital.

I somehow made it (and would look out into the parking lot each day at my Nova and wonder how I actually got there). I was in the ER briefly, but when they heard the word "hallucination," I was jammed into a wheelchair and deposited at the admissions desk of "R-5." I knew R-5 from my statistical work, and I knew it was easier to get in than to get out. I announced to the reception nurse that it was a mistake, that I was fine, and that I was leaving. As I stood up, two big guys held me as one stuck a hypodermic needle in my butt: Thorazine. My struggle to leave was over, and I woke up in a hospital bed about 4:00 the next morning.

Memories of that hospitalization are not at all clear. Just vignettes. I remember the mindless exercise song *Chicken Fat* that we slogged through pathetically each morning. I remember a visit from the assistant administrative director of Dunn reassuring me that he had created a fictive identity for me so my coworkers would not learn of my residence on R-5. (Another deep irony: Community Mental Health protecting me from the shame and stigma of…Community Mental Health.)

I do remember the first visit from a Dunn staff psychiatrist, that first Saturday morning (and he wasn't the one we knew as the *good one*).

"Sometimes, like now, you feel very sad, no?"

"*Uh, yes.*"

"And sometimes you feel very happy—almost too happy, no?" Had to think about that one. Maybe, like when I started with a new college, or ostensibly a new life. "Garry, it's not your fault. You suffer from bipolar disorder. We have a great drug for that, lithium. It's natural, like a salt. And it will change your life."

I protested: "Tried it before, and it did nothing. Except side effects. I was constantly thirsty. And gained a lot of weight. I don't want side effects."

"Garry, side effects are a given…the only medicines I have with no side effects are placebos—you know what placebos are?"

"Uh, yes."

"But there is something new with almost no side effects, it's not approved for your condition yet but it's promising, and it's called carbamazepine. It's used for seizures, but the patients who take it report feeling happier."

"No side effects?"

"Well, not in most cases. But you need to have regular blood tests to check for irreversible effects."

"But no weight gain? No thirst and peeing all the time?"

"No. Nothing like that. And the side effects are very rare, very rare."

"OK, Let's do it."

I stayed in the hospital for twelve days, and actually became reasonably comfortable with the routine, starting each morning with *Chicken Fat* and ending with some unidentified sleep aid. Perhaps too comfortable, as one evening the charge nurse stunned me with: "I know your diagnosis. Your diagnosis is 'I don't want to go to work and I like free meals.' Seems we always have at least one of your kind here."

I knew three things at that point.

1. There was nothing magical about hospitalization—I felt about as depressed as I had when I entered.

2. Carbamazepine was doing nothing, at least at this point.

3. If I was ever going to get better—undepressed—I would need to take responsibility. There was no magic. But I had no idea how I was going to do it. Or how excruciatingly long it would take.

Addendum to College
(Between Earlham and Stockton)

Harvard Extension

My lifelong friend, Phil, was worried about me—and my mental health. An MIT junior, he invited me up to spend a few days with him in his group house in Cambridge. It was a real schizoid scene: MIT and Harvard students studying like their lives depended on it; then partying like their lives would end tomorrow. I loved it. Dinners were especially fascinating. One evening, some house alums and recent MIT grads brought their latest project as food engineers for General Foods: new, more powerful Pop Rocks. Pop Rocks with chasers from a pony keg of Narragansett: This was a better way to live!

One of the Harvard students gave me the best possible tip: you could attend night school at Harvard (Harvard Extension) without going through any acceptance process. Just register, pay the tuition, and you're taught by regular Harvard faculty. I was entranced. My college conundrum was solved while drinking the local brew—in the epicenter of American letters. A depression cure for sure.

The semester was about to begin, so I rushed home to New Jersey, packed up the 1969 Dodge "Swinger" with all my books, and headed out to say my goodbyes. My first stop was Branch's house—Branch, of the ill-fated geodesic dome project in Maine. The Swinger was very hard to start, so I left it running as I knocked on his door. In the door glass I could see my car inching away, in reverse. My first sense was if someone wanted to steal a '69 Dodge, they needed it more than I did. But turning around, I saw that no one was driving the car. And it was backing down toward the biggest hill in Haddonfield, New Jersey.

I sprang into action: caught up with the car, and opened the door. Running alongside, I reached for the gear shift (which had apparently vibrated from Park to Reverse). As I held on to the shifter, the open door knocked me down and my hand pulled the lever to Drive. The car continued in reverse and ran over my leg. The transmission made a god-awful sound of crunching and grinding, then the car came back toward me in Drive and ran over both legs! It glanced off a tree and took out part of the porch on a now not-fully-lovely 19th century Victorian.

The ambulance came when a neighbor called and noted that a man seemed to have been run over by his own car. My mother, who monitored all risks in the community on a perpetually-on police scanner, said to herself, "That has to be Garry."

At the ER they were quite surprised that there were no breaks. But when they cut my pants off, my legs blew up like Jersey watermelons. Severe sprains. I would be on crutches for at least two to three weeks. And no more Dodge Swinger. Harvard was off. My depression deepened.

Hospital, Part 2

I would go for stretches—sometimes months—where I would not be on any psych meds at all. Those were generally periods of "isms," where I tested my latest (desperate) theories of what could free me from depression's grip. Vegetarianism. Buddhism. Abstinence-ism. Academism.

None was more effective than the other, but I, more often than not, blamed myself for not being "ism" enough.

In graduate school at the University of Iowa (communication studies and academism), I discovered, through a pretty skilled clinical social worker, Aaron Beck and cognitive therapy. Read the textbook preface to endnotes, and became a devotee to the cognitive triad. I could out-Beck Beck. I read Albert Ellis and considered what Beck may have borrowed from him. Read psychiatrist David Burns (a Beck acolyte). I even interviewed at the University of Iowa School of Social Work: I could make a career of this stuff.

As with all my isms, this one lost its sheen when it just didn't do the job. I was becoming depressed about being depressed: no matter how obsessively I would complete my Beck diagrams and syllogisms, my scores on the *Beck Depression Index* and the *Scale for Suicidal Ideation* were increasing.

I was working with a therapist, Blanche, at the time, after my relationship with the Beck-acolyte social worker devolved into a series of weekly debates. Blanche was legend in Iowa City: a Birmingham, Alabama debutante who ran away to the Esalen institute in the '60s, danced naked overlooking the Pacific with Fritz Perls, and in the process gained an M.A. in counseling. She practiced an eclectic synthesis of Freud, gestalt and Maslow-based self-actualization, and she never lost her genuine Birmingham upper-crust lilt.

A new ism, Blanche-ism. We explored my artistic side. She cautioned me that "the worst form of alienation is alienation from the self." It made good sense. I was depressed because I had closeted my artistic self after leaving art school (college #2, Temple University's Tyler School of Art). The problem with this theory was kind of simple: I was so depressed in art school I dropped out after a year (despite producing some noteworthy work).

Desperate, and feeling crushed by a demanding course load and teaching responsibilities, I made an appointment with the student health psychiatrist.

I went in with notes: "I'm exhausted. I can't concentrate. I don't feel smart enough to be in my program. I don't want to get out of bed. And I feel guilty about all of this."

"You forgot a few: Appetite. Obsession with health. Loss of libido."

"But I don't feel those things…"

"Listen, the medications we give here aren't amphetamines—you know, *speed*. You come in with a not-even memorized list of symptoms so I'll give you something that will help you study, or whatever. That's not what I do. I think this session is over."

I crashed from that point. Deeper into depression, I stopped going to classes. I somehow walked through my teaching responsibilities. But three days later, I became immobilized. I had a panic attack in the supermarket across the street where I lived. I ran across the street to my latest residence, a bank building a friend and I rented after it went under during the farm crisis (my mother wasn't the only one who fantasized about the power of a different address). I had my hat, gloves, heavy coat on, lying on my bed, unable to move even enough to remove my gloves. My phone rang and rang.

After about an hour (that's a rough guess, as my sense of time was "off"—could have been more evidence for the good doctor at student health) my roommate Luanne showed up. She was a dancer and kind of a professional "artist in residence" who also did movement therapy at community mental health, and was pretty psych-wise. "I'm taking you to University Hospital."

"No, not there! I don't want to have anything to do with that place."

"But it's a really good hospital..."

"Their doctors suck."

"OK, OK, I'll take you to Memorial" (the community hospital).

All along the snowy drive from Solon, Iowa (population 720, twenty miles north of Iowa City) to Memorial, I kept asking, "Does Blanche know?" "Yes, Blanche knows." "Are you sure Blanche knows?"

We arrived at Memorial around midnight. Problem: they didn't have a psych ward, and said they would call an ambulance to transport me to U of I Hospital. I refused. So they put me in a private room, where I stayed for ten days.

I had lots of visitors: friends, students, Blanche. And the resident psychiatrist, who put me on nortriptyline. No instant effects, but in a few weeks' time, it actually helped. I gained weight and wobbled when I stood up. A more-than-reasonable tradeoff for being able to resume my studies and my teaching.

Not much more to say about the hospitalization. I could have had the same experience at a better hotel. No "chicken fat." No "frequent flyer roommate." Just visitors. TV reruns. And nortriptyline.

Symptoms

S lowing down. It all starts with slowing down. As if there's a speed control on my back, and someone is turning the dial back. And as it turns, the rate of slowing increases. It's a complete slowing: thinking, speaking—even moving. My depressions always begin with slowing down.

At the same time, a cruel inversion takes place. The things that bring me joy in the well times first degenerate to no positive reaction. But as time—and slowing—pass, the flat response slips into aversion. So: reading; sailing; even The Beatles, now generate a negative, even repulsive reaction. A doctor once characterized this as "anhedonia." I suggested it was more like "anti-hedonia," if that's a word.

Slow thinking breeds negative obsessions with every-thing, including myself. I'm not *this* enough and not *that* enough. My accomplishments, modest as they are, are somehow flukes. Which leads to guilt feelings. Soon, the depressive thoughts about myself "globalize," and nihil-ism takes over my thinking.

Paradoxically, many well-intentioned therapeutic processes reinforce, rather than relieve, these symptoms. Cognitive approaches make me feel un-smart. Group therapy can make me feel undeserving of my own com-plaints. Mindfulness exercises can make me feel deeper in the moment that I'm trying to escape. And starting back on meds can feel like a crapshoot where the odds are not at all with me.

Unsurprisingly, what David Burns refers to as "do-nothing-ism" is my primary behavioral response to all of this. I sleep to excess, sometimes fourteen or more hours a day. And this despite my fear of sleeping as it brings violent, or at least nihilistic, nightmares (and daymares). Getting out of bed in the morning requires several steps of pre-engineering the night before: coffee-pot on the timer, two (or three) alarm clocks in different rooms. Sleeping in my clothes is reserved for the worst periods.

Why I haven't just given in and given up in these deep depressions is not clear to me.

Psychiatrists— and Meds—of Note

T he self-help literature likes to cover itself with the suggestion that you "... seek the input of a qualified psychologist or psychiatrist." Some go further and admonish the patient to find a therapist with whom they have a solid rapport. The simple arithmetic—too many patients; too few mental health professionals—makes this nostrum, at best, unrealistic. And the hegemony of the insurance companies over the entire spectrum of mental health care limits choices further. The result is not surprising: if you're lucky enough to find care, rapport is more likely an accident than a plan.

With this as a backdrop, I'll outline several cases where I found such good fortune prior to, or between, hospitalizations.

Dr. G., 1980: After the Richmond, Indiana, hospital stay, I returned home to live with my folks—briefly, I hoped. I contacted the local community mental health center in neighboring Cherry Hill, New Jersey. Dr. G. was in his 60s and had no doubt seen it all. But he hadn't grown cynical (a trait I saw when I worked in the community mental health center setting). Instead, his was a curmudgeonly but kind simplicity that raised my feeling of trust. I remember our first session, when he noted with some incredulity, "You are really depressed. It's a mystery why no one ever tried you on ANTI-depressants."

He wrote a prescription for amitriptyline and set an appointment for the next week. I pretty quickly became the walking catalog of classic tricyclic side effects: sweating, dizziness, dry mouth, and a funky one—a strange, acidic taste in my mouth. It took about three weeks to experience any therapeutic effects, but when it began, it bordered on glorious. It was spring; for once in my life I wasn't working; and I was learning that medication *could* help me. After the experiences of lithium (twice) and carbamazepine, I had little confidence in medical treatments. That was changing. I took long walks—just because I *could*, and it felt good. Each week brought more improvements—subtle at first, but building toward a level of wellbeing that I could not remember experiencing.

Dr. G. was visibly delighted, but the insurance company less so. I was reaching the end of my coverage, and the side effects were not abating. Weight was creeping up. He cautioned me against going off the amitriptyline and wrote for several refills. As I sat in his office I wondered if I was going to take his uncharacteristically stern guidance. It was not the warmest note to close our relationship on.

A few weeks later I was traveling to see friends back in Indiana. I stopped for the night in Breezewood, PA— proudly promoted as "the town of motels." My room was a borderline-frightening mishmash of pseudo-Tudor and purples and chartreuses. Somehow each of my side-effects was intensifying. Especially the acidic taste. I flushed the bottle of amitriptyline down the purple toilet. Then I panicked, hearing Dr. G.'s closing admonition in my head.

Over the next few days, I felt shaky. And scared. And yes, my depression re-emerged with startling alacrity.

Dr. I., 1985: Dr. I. was approaching retirement from a private practice in Iowa City, Iowa. He was finishing out his career as a part-time psychiatrist at the local community mental health center. I was never really sure if his film-like absent-mindedness was a "technique" (like the "stumblebum technique" some statistics professors use to check if the class is awake). Or simply authentic. In either case, it was a highly collaborative relationship. We collectively explored my diagnosis (major depression, recurring—with or without psychotic features was the question). And we considered the risk/benefits of meds. Not sure how we settled on imipramine, but I started it right away. Felt lightheaded on standing. And started gaining weight at a rate that eclipsed the amitriptyline. Dr. I. encouraged me to stay the course, and I did. He would always bring it back to a simple risk/benefit equation. The tradeoff was clear, and the answer obvious. I *was* feeling better.

Dr. I. retired fully in the middle of my treatment. At that point, I had my first experience with the "I feel fine, I don't need these meds" syndrome. And I quit—not as dramatically as I had at the motel in Breezewood; I unceremoniously put the bottle of pills away in a kitchen cabinet. I did eventually toss them in the trash to reinforce my sense that I could do it by myself, naturally.

I learned that medical history tends to rhyme, as some claim political history does. In a matter of days I sensed the return of my depressive sensations. Now I had a dilemma—go back to the imipramine with the side effects and (irrational) tension that "I shouldn't have to take meds." Or prove to myself that I could manage depression without them. I chose plan B. It was not successful. This led to a protracted depression that peaked in about a month's time, and sent me to the Student Health psychiatrist who accused me of trying to procure "speed."

Dr. J. 1990: This was a relatively short encounter, once again, driven by insurance limitations.

I saw Dr. J. on the referral of a cognitive therapist I was working with after I first moved to Baltimore. Dr. J. was youngish, a kind of "cool doc" with lots of the appropriate props in his office (don't remember specifically, but African art?). I liked his relaxed approach—he asked great questions and actually listened to the answers. When he asked how I managed my dreadful mornings, I announced—with some self-consciousness—that I drank two pots of coffee to get myself going. He thought for a couple of minutes, then asked: "Did you ever try an MAOI?"

"No—never even heard of it."

"Well, an MAOI is a very old drug, like from the 1950s. It was seen as a miracle drug until a very serious and potential side effect was discovered—a dangerous spike in blood pressure when certain foods are consumed." He explained the tyramine reaction, and listed the forbidden foods and drink.

I said, "I can do that." And I left with a prescription for phenelzine.

Phenelzine, in short, was awesome. I had initiative, energy, optimism. I looked forward to the mornings. I would get up at 4 a.m. or so, eat breakfast, go for a run, come home and eat breakfast #2. That was the dawning of a problem. I was constantly hungry, and my weight rose from 145 to 165, to 175, to 190. I bought all new clothes—twice. And still they didn't fit.

Still, the trade-off seemed worth it. I was productive—started a business, got married, learned to sail. Things I'd fantasized about in my less-depressed days when I could still fantasize. I checked in periodically with Dr. J. He suggested I try to switch to another MAOI, tranylcypromine. Less potential for weight gain. But it wasn't as effective. I went back to phenelzine after a few weeks.

One night, after directing a twelve-hour video shoot, I went to an Italian restaurant for a late dinner and ordered a salad with no cheese. I was just so tired and hungry I dug into the salad without thinking. About halfway through realized why it tasted so terrific—it was made with cheese. I asked the server, and she said, "Well, yes, what's the big deal?" A big deal it was.

I left a twenty on the table, ran to my car, and set out for home. Driving on the beltway my neck stiffened to the point where I could not turn my head to watch traffic. This was soon accompanied by the most powerful, percussive headache I ever had. I spotted one of those hospital "H" signs and exited and followed the signs to Metropolitan Hospital. I left my car in the portico—could not remember if it was running or not—and went inside to explain what was happening to me. I was put on a gurney and ignored for an excruciating period of time, which I cannot estimate now. Finally, I shouted, "Take my goddamn blood pressure." They did, and their shock was clear. They gave me something, and I was out.

The next day, the phenelzine found itself in the toilet. The weight rolled off. And, of course, the depression rolled back.

And two that went sour...

Dr. V., 1992: I had a novel introduction to Dr. V. —I met him at a party. He was just starting his practice and was keen to add patients. We spent a little time discussing his approach: client-centered and eclectic. Not doctrinaire, and certainly not cognitive. My optimism soared. Our early sessions were dynamic—he respected my perspectives and unearthed my potential. Medically, he started me on bupropion. Bupropion was a different animal: no discernible side effects other than constipation. Modest relief of depressive symptoms. Seemed like a more-than-reasonable tradeoff. And that, along with Dr. V.'s assurances that "the universe wants you to succeed," was enough to keep me coming back. And keep me taking that bupropion.

I've learned that a reasonable target for depression patients is 80 percent better, 80 percent of the time. Dr. V. seemed to be more of a 60/60 practitioner. I felt pretty good, much of the time. Yet it didn't come close to the stunning success of phenelzine. I had the inner sense that I *could* do better. I grew frustrated.

At the same time, I felt Dr. V.'s growing frustration with me. He would take about half of our sessions to discuss the stock market and seemed to want stock tips from me (investment management being my field). I was determined to stay with the bupropion—my lesson about stopping had been learned, viscerally, more than once.

So I stayed the medication course, but looked for a new doctor.

Dr. Z., 1994: I can't remember how I found Dr. Z., but he seemed like the anti-Dr. V. He practiced a modified cognitive approach that focused on the stories we tell ourselves. Change—or at least modify—those stories, and you can change your life. Indeed, we worked from a book called *Reinventing Your Life*. "Brains are stupid," he liked to say, "they believe what we tell them." I was ready for a more structured approach, and one in which the word "universe" did not emerge. We did good work with this model—I just reviewed some of my notes from that period and saw the insights that emerged.

My basic story—relentless depression and failure—did not hold up to the scrutiny Dr. Z. and I applied. In truth my personal history was more balanced, and I had succeeded at a number of things *despite* the recurring depressions.

We agreed that bupropion was not fully doing the job, so he tried me on a series of SSRIs, starting with paroxetine, and moving through the list. All had some effect in reducing my depression: slightly more so than bupropion. I still, however, measured every med against phenelzine and was consistently disappointed.

Disappointment eased into our therapy as well. The book was a revelation, and I captured my frequent insights in emails to Dr. Z. Not tomes, these were two-, three-, and four-sentence thoughts that I wanted to capture and use to frame our next sessions. At one of these, he noted, sternly, "I don't have time to read your emails, and I don't get paid to do it. If you have concerns, bring them to the session, got it?" Perhaps I overreacted. But I felt the rapport we had built was damaged. Those emails were a critical part of my healing—healing, in some cases, of decades-long conflicts with myself. I continued to see Dr. Z. for a couple more sessions, asked for a longer-term prescription for sertraline, and walked out for the last time.

A mixed bag:

Dr. B., 1999: Dr. B. did group therapy exclusively. A devotee of group therapy pioneer Irvin Yalom, MD, of Stanford, Dr. B. ran a number of groups, primarily for young professionals in Baltimore. He had the remarkable ability to draw people out in a group setting, even those who were most reticent, or most in pain. The rawness in that big room of fifteen or so was palpable, but so was the sense of safety. Most helpful to me was seeing others who were in the throes of depression but remained worthwhile, likeable, people, with something to contribute. I was forced to conclude that must be true for myself as well. I heard the stories they told themselves and could only hope that my own stories were equally distorted, too negative, to be accurate descriptions of reality. I looked forward to weekly group. For an hour I was apart from the judging world and immersed in a place of acceptance.

The downside: Dr. B.'s model was that group was *the* answer. Only it wasn't mine, at least not fully. My depression was deepening as my insights grew. I felt I needed to go along with the group's ethos that we were all getting better, at least incrementally. I was still attending when I collapsed completely at work, and found myself sobbing under my desk.

Other Things
That Didn't Work

A wise psychiatrist once cautioned me against "the trap of meaning." By this, she meant that those with recurrent, biologically based major depression often look for clear pathways of cause and effect. It's a trap, because major depression can strike in the best of times as well as the worst of times. It can strike the ascetic just as it can strike the self-indulgent. I guess that pursuing (the trap of) meaning gives the illusion that you can control depression if you can only find what switches it off. I wasted a lot of emotional energy, brainpower, and time looking for that switch.

Inestimable hours of talk therapy, as I observed earlier, did not give me the sustained relief that I desperately wanted. And I set out to find the answer in books: self-help books, professional tomes, even medical textbooks. I still have a collection from different periods in my life: college, working life, grad school, and beyond. Yet in my depressed state, the impact of these volumes ranged from none whatsoever, to the intensification of my symptoms.

The most destructive (and I use that word quite intentionally) to my sense of self were the ones that posited depression as completely non-biological. Everything from the promotion of mindfulness cures to medical practitioners who disparaged the medical model, slowly eroded my sense of self. Did I *want* to be depressed? Was it motivated by the "secondary gains" that can be part of depression (sympathy, low expectations, limited responsibility)? I doubted myself. Which, of course, intensified my depression.

I found myself reading and rereading a passage from a highly popular and broadly respected psychiatrist, in which he told the story of a young woman who refused to give up her depression. He had done his best for her as a first-rate therapist, but she stubbornly adhered to her depressive state. Could that be my problem? Did I, in some perverse and self-serving way, *want* to feel this way? How could I know that I didn't?

So books were not especially helpful, especially the self-help variety.

Friends could also—with the best of intentions—intensify my dis-ease. Bromides, such as "you have so much going for you," or "there are people (in the third world, et al.) who would trade places with you in a minute." Or the worst: "I was depressed once when Rover died, but I pulled myself out of it. You can do it, too." This alienated me from those I was closest to. Clearly they did not comprehend my experience. So did they really know me?

I even, in my desperation, sought the guidance of a psychic who was a retired physician. He went into a trance and reported that Baltimore was not the place for me and that I might find relief in a new community, Richmond, Virginia. It was striking that he chose that destination, as I had visited there recently and experienced little of the heralded Southern hospitality. This reminded me of the guidance I received from my therapist Blanche, who thought my answer was to return to art school. That turned out to be a place where I really struggled.

My most extreme attempt at finding mental health was my abstinence from every ordinary source of pleasure. Not just what you're thinking—sexual activity. Alcohol, caffeine, even sugar. I stopped listening to The Beatles—perhaps the most extreme self-deprivation. In short, I lived a monkish existence for several months, without the advantages conferred by a monastery.

Not surprisingly, this approach was a disaster. The more "pure" I became, the more excruciating my standards grew. I was not a whole lot of fun to hang out with at this time, either, so my friends called less and less.

I almost laugh at myself when I remember this period—I was in my late twenties, and tried it again after my divorce in my early fifties. But I can't laugh as it brings into painful high relief just how troubled and lost I was. And was, more or less, for decades.

One more "technique" I tried at a number of junctures: journaling. This, allegedly, would allow you to purge your dark thoughts by capturing them, thus gaining rational distance. I would capture my thoughts, not censoring or diluting. It was frightening what would come out of me. Self-blame, self-loathing. And occasionally the desire to not exist. Even when my depression was at a relatively subdued level—which it was, at times—the things I would say about myself and my life were truly disturbing. Anyone who knew me, even those who knew me well, would likely be shocked—as if it were someone else being channeled. I guess in a sense it was. My underlying, disturbed self.

I would launch one of these projects, be it a new book or a new routine, with the blind faith that this would be the key. This is surprising, given my track record with such projects (miserable), and the depth of my despair. But like changing colleges, or my mother changing addresses, hope and the placebo effect were seductive.

Hospital, Part 3

I felt it for probably two weeks: slowing down. Knowing what was happening, I made an appointment with my company's HR representative to alert her to what was most likely coming: an immobilizing depression. We agreed to keep the lines of communication open, but the morning that things fell apart, the HR rep was at an off-campus meeting.

I don't remember the exact choreography, but my assistant at my job in a major investment firm found me in my darkened office, under my desk, alternately weeping softly and sobbing uncontrollably. She called the HR rep back to the office, and it was she who drove me to Johns Hopkins.

When I arrived, there was no room in the psych ward, so I was temporarily admitted to a room in the general hospital. I was first visited by a social worker who assured me that the staff was well-versed in cognitive behavioral therapy and that would be all I needed to beat my depression. I feebly tried to debate her, but she insisted.

Some time passed, and a psychiatry resident, Dr. H., came to see me. He didn't diagnose me, or preview my treatment, but did reassure me that Hopkins would use all its resources to get me well again. He personally wheeled me to the psych unit, where I slept in my room for probably an hour or two. By this point, Dr. H. said he had to go on night shift, but he would be in first thing to see me when he got off. I thought, he's a nice man, but I won't see him again, and drifted off to sleep. Next morning, I woke about 6:00, and at 7:00, I saw the silhouette of a large man in my doorway. It was Dr. H. Wow, a promise kept. Kinda new to my hospital experience.

Later that morning I was interviewed, in my pajamas and IV pole, by a roomful of doctors, sitting in a circle in a too-small office. We went through my symptoms, and they jotted notes. Several of the questions seemed to be checking for manic episodes. When they got to the suicide "series," I could tell I really had their attention.

At this time, there were a series of shootings at gas stations in Northern Virginia. They seemed to follow some kind of pattern, or so the police believed. So I bought a street map of the area, plotted the shootings, and tried to predict where they would hit next. In my state, I somehow felt that if I could place myself at the "right" place at the "right" time, I would be the next victim. Passive suicide.

One doctor, who closed the meeting with the words, "Mr. Cosnett, I think you're really depressed," garnered nods from the other docs.

I don't remember much about the daily activities in the unit, but I did try to participate authentically. After a couple of days they took me to watch a video on electroconvulsive therapy (ECT). I felt such empathy for the patient in the video that I sat and cried until someone took me back to the unit. That afternoon a doctor asked me if I wanted to proceed with ECT, and based on the promise the video offered, I said yes.

Later that day, I was visited in my room by an anesthesiologist, who seemed to me like she was about 17 years old. She reviewed the risks. I didn't care. Some almost sounded attractive. I signed the release.

Two mornings later, they put me and my IV on a gurney, took me down the elevator, and sat me outside the ECT suite. After what was probably a half hour, I was wheeled into a ghastly, tight, paneled room and lay there waiting. And waiting.

Finally, I was wheeled into another too-tight room, now with Dr. C., the anesthesiologist, and another doctor. The room was just plain scary, with instruments and electronics, and beeps, and sucking sounds. To distract myself, I started a conversation and accelerated it as the propofol started to take effect, but the propofol won. Next thing I knew, of course, I was in recovery, and I was taken back to breakfast in the ward.

The doctors had projected, I believe, eight treatments, but after three I started to show surprising improvement, and they completed the course at five. ECT and I got along especially well (which would not be my experience years later), and I felt I was watching myself get my life back. I was.

After a few days I met with a social worker who offered some solid, practical guidance, and set up my first outpatient appointment with Dr. H. The HR representative came to take me home. I must have slept for eighteen hours. But I was home. And I *wanted* to get up.

Four weeks later, I was working in the London office of my employer. Essentially symptom free. And, of course, taking my "Hopkins Special" (nortriptyline and lithium).

Work

After my experiences with house painting and home repair sent me running back to the academy, I resolved never again to earn my living through manual labor. My brain, when it was working, seemed to be my best tool for supporting myself.

"How would you like to take a break before you write your dissertation and teach at a little college in Baltimore?" asked Lauren, a colleague from my Iowa Ph.D. program. That sounded pretty perfect. I had just passed my qualifying exams and was exhausted from my recent hospitalization (#2), and weary of the unrelenting pressure of the program. Two days later I was on a plane to Baltimore, and two days after that I was on the plane back to Iowa as assistant professor of communication arts.

I was not prepared for the cool reception that I received from the Iowa faculty, upon learning of my "success." My advisor warned me: "Small colleges are not about finding truth, as we are here in our program." A former professor was more direct: taking me out to lunch, he revealed his disappointment with the first beer. "We didn't train you in the Iowa method so that you would go out and... TEACH." With a nauseating spin on the word "teach."

I was starting to think I would never return to that coercive truth-seeking environment called, somewhat ironically, "Communication Studies." After all, I had an academic job already—tenure track. I packed my belongings into my wheezing 1972 BMW and headed east.

The misalignment between the college and me revealed itself early. A group of faculty members took me out for drinks, and in a disturbing round-robin recited the number of intro courses they had left to teach until retirement. Jeez, my number at that point was incalculable. Besides, I liked teaching intro courses.

A series of small yet disturbing encounters like this got me worrying that maybe the professors back at Iowa were right. In my escape from the pressures of the academy, I'd retreated to the pressures of a (very) "small town." Small towns are not known for the pursuit of truth through vigorous, learned dialogue. And I was to learn, with one gasp, I wasn't in Iowa anymore.

The college hosted the innovative (in the '50s and '60s) and highly prized Yale filmmaker, Faith Hubley. After a film screening for the entire college, the president asked for questions. In such situations, the waiting is painful. I decided to take the initiative (and relieve the tension) with my most sincere inquiry:

"How do I give my students access to the meaning of your work when the first question they are likely to ask is how much did the editor get paid?"

An audible gasp from the president. No mistaking it. Audible back to row 15. I certainly can overreact to negative stimuli, but if anything, I underestimated the consequences here. From that moment on, I could do no right. That was made clear by the president and her acolytes.

I survived another year, but it was clear that tenure was not in my future. Nor was intellectual fulfillment.

So I asked to be transferred to the Adult Division. Evening and weekend courses for working adults. And it was wonderful. They were motivated students who were grateful to have a chance (or second chance) at college.

My favorite course was "Writing for College." It was designed for those who met all the criteria for admission except passing the writing test. Alternatively, they had to pass this course in their first semester to continue. Traditionally, the pass rate was around 70 percent. My target was 100 percent. And I accomplished that. I broke everything down to the fundamentals, made extensive comments and corrections on every essay, and told the class repeatedly that our collective goal was everyone passes.

Well, by meeting this goal I was immediately seen as a grade inflator. It was "impossible" that everyone passed; that never happens. I presented evidence: a lovely Christmas essay sent to me by the man who struggled the hardest in the class. I was given the privilege of teaching for another year, which I did. But the depression that had sent me to the hospital three years earlier, was showing itself again. I was slowing down.

I was running a bit of a race with myself. Could I make it two more semesters before the depression overwhelmed me? I was seeing a psychiatrist at the time (Dr. V.) and taking bupropion. It was enough of a therapeutic combination to keep my head above water—barely, at times. I did make it through, although the grueling schedule of teaching multiple courses and maintaining my perfect record of no student failures was impossible to continue. I surrendered my post.

Earlier, when I was full-time faculty, the college wanted to turn me into a profit center and had me do public workshops on presentation skills ("Overcome Podium Panic with Prof. Garry Cosnett"). People were paying $250 for a full-day program. It occurred to me that the college was grossing around $3,000 for each of these and paying me $600. If I could do it on my own, I could make some serious money. Further, I could work when I was well, and not work when I wasn't.

Banks were flush at this time—right before the banking crash—and I approached the big ones with an offer of $2,000 Investment Communication Seminars, which sounded more substantial. I got a couple of clients right off, and discovered that I knew the drill so well, I could pull it off even when somewhat depressed. For thirteen years the model worked, even during a number of really down times. I just wouldn't book work when depression took over.

Then 9/11 and the Great Recession ate away at my business model. So when my largest client, a major investment firm, offered me a full-time position, I did not hesitate.

The work I do for them, investment communication, requires intense concentration. I review investment reports, generally 20+ pages with millions of dollars—or more—in the balance. It's rewarding work. I have terrific colleagues—the investment analysts—and I have a demonstrable effect on their success. And by extension, the success of the company. I am paid well, but more important, appreciated for my contribution. This gives me latitude to bring my full self to work.

When another bout of depression started to slow me down, I was scared—really scared. I would read page two of the report, and not be able to remember page one. At my worst, I would read paragraph two and not be able to remember what paragraph one said. I was on my way to hospitalization #3, as described in the previous chapter.

After successful ECT treatments, I was back at work a month after I entered the hospital, and working in the London office three weeks later.

I am grateful to my HR rep, who drove me to the hospital, admitted me, and stayed "… until I see your name on a room." She informed my boss and gave him a mini-teach-in on depression and its biological underpinnings. I would receive encouraging emails from my boss every couple of days after that, and reassurance that my job was safely waiting for me.

The same story unfolded four years later. Only more severe, on every dimension. Hospitalization #4. No miraculous response to ECT. Temporary delirium. I missed an entire quarter of work. And when I came back, I was running at probably 70 percent of my former capacity. The firm stood by me, supported me, and let me find my own pace back. I am, again, grateful.

There have been ups and downs, ebbs and flows, since then. I do worry that I may have to take leave from work one time too many. My goal is to work several more years—to age 70. When work works for me, it is deeply rewarding. I have impact. And appreciation. It does take its toll and is probably young(er) person's work. Yet I wake up most mornings looking forward to plying my trade and making a difference.

This reminds me of an encounter I had with a psychiatrist during hospitalization #3. I said, with full sincerity:

"You're a very nice person, and I appreciate that. But you and I both know that I'll never work another day in my life."

"Mr. Cosnett, no, I don't know that. I don't know that at all. I do know that it's your depression talking."

She was right.

Relationships

As an investor, I understand that believing "this time is different" is a dangerous assumption. Entering into new romantic relationships, however, I applied this optimistic approach, with few exceptions. I clung to the unexamined assumption that a new relationship—like my mother's new neighborhood—held the key to overcoming my depression.

This pattern started early. Freshman year of college, I met a bona fide preppy. (Not the wannabes I knew from my public high school.) Boarding school-attending, horseback-riding, trust-funding child of privilege, with two middle names! "Mills" was a bit of a hippie, too. A very rich hippie. But with peasant shirts, jeans that were worn in the right places, work boots, and a David Bowie haircut. Girl of my dreams, and she was interested in me. We were introduced orientation week and were fairly stuck together from that point on.

The attraction was immediate, and the bond of affection soon followed. We talked about art, politics (lefty), and the educational system (she planned to be an alternative-school teacher).

In the excitement of a new (and cross-cultural) relationship, free-floating depression was pushed to the margins of my consciousness. Love was all it could be to my 18-year-old mind, and somehow intensified by the stark contrast in our backgrounds.

That salutary effect on my depression did not continue. The more I learned about Mills, the less adequate I felt. Her parents, who had come from multiple generations of American wealth, were philanthropists and supporters of the arts. They had live-in "help," two vacation homes, and a ranch. Add to that impeccable Ivy League credentials going back generations (*they* met in Palm Beach on semester break). Upon meeting me, they concluded, "Garry is a very nice boy, but he's not one of us." As I came to see clearly, I was not.

At the same time, my growing insecurity and obsessive need for reassurance was becoming the centerpiece of our relationship. Whereas I first saw Mills as the cure for my depression, a gestalt shift took place. She was now the *source* of my depressed feelings. Her successes, friends, and high-status family had become thorns in my sense of self. The more I learned, the less adequate I felt to be Mills's mate.

The contrast in cultures came into high relief when her parents announced they were coming to meet with my parents to discuss our relationship. Terror was the best way to describe my parents' reaction to that news. "I don't know how to talk to a millionaire," my father protested. My mother's response was, "I can't deal with this—you have to tell them not to come."

They did come, and the discomfort on both sides was palpable. Mills's parents kept scanning the little twelve-by-twelve living room, with the fake brick wall on which my middle school shop project, a cast aluminum eagle on a mahogany shield, presided. It was like they were anthropologists discovering a lost tribe—*Do people actually live this way?* Her parents were tongue tied. "Was that your high school we passed? How is the science department?" Anything was discussed but the relationship between Mills and Garry.

Mercifully, the ordeal was brief. The parents blurted that they had to take an earlier flight, but asked me to follow them to the airport. At that awkward goodbye nothing was said of the visit, but Mills's dad blurted, "You know, Mills, this is killing your grandmother." Driving back home, my depression tested new limits.

The relationship was running on fumes at that point. What was so clearly my escape route through depression at the outset now became a near-unbearable intensifier of it.

I cannot honestly remember who ended it first, but there were a few hopeless reunions before the final end came. Mills took some time off from school and worked for one of her family's businesses. I returned to my family's home and reverted to my go-to in such situations: house painting and odd jobs.

Looking back, it's clear that my depression was the proximate cause of this relationship's collision course. Lawyers ask the "but for" question to determine responsibility. But for my depression, I could have managed the cross-cultural stresses. At her core, Mills was a kind, loving, and generous soul, who happened to love me. Until I became unlovable.

Fast forward through a number of other relationships: the townie, the cult-deprogrammer, the academic. The same pattern fell into place, always on a similar schedule of excitement eclipsing depression, followed by signs it was creeping back in (constant need for reassurance was a critical sign), then the belief that it was the relationship itself that was causing the depression. In no case was "this time different."

My final relationship before Kristin was with Kelli. Kelli was both clever and attractive, and a skilled flirt. We met in a local book club, and agreed to have an Indian dinner (both our faves) to share dating horror stories. This was probably dangerous territory, because through the evening, each of us looked less and less like the disasters we had come from. It proved to be the launching of the relationship.

Kelli was ten years younger, obsessed with sports, and athletic. I was fifty, and yoga was my sport, and I struggled to keep up with her and her friends on the soccer field. Her most-recent boyfriend commonly joined the games, and he certainly came with ample grounds for jealousy. He was tall and athletic, with that unruly soccer-player hair. I felt like someone's father.

To complete the pattern, depression emerged, this time with real force. I told Kelli that I didn't have anything to give her. And I was right. Within weeks of our breakup, I was in the hospital for hospitalization #3.

Finally—perhaps because I had sworn off dating—I could point to lessons learned from this experience. But as with my colleges, or my mother's houses, the seeds of depression were in the new situation. What began as my cure transformed—slowly at first—into my undoing. Like the medications that first seemed so promising and then disappointed, relationships to me were like novel pharmaceuticals. They worked for a while but wore off quickly.

I met Kristin when I was closing in on sixty. I had intentionally avoided dating for a couple years in hopes of getting some kind of perspective on why and how my relationships followed the same pattern. I can be a slow learner when it comes to my own behavior, and nowhere is this more true than relationships. But I did, in that period of reflection, recognize the pattern. And had to give up the fantasy that a relationship—the right one with "the right one"—would deliver me to the promised land of mental health.

Armed with this hard-won insight, I entered my relationship with Kristin with a promise to myself (and to Kristin), not to make our relationship about my depression. This is tricky at times, and I'm not always successful. At times it sneaks up on me. But I'm vigilant, and I know what to look and feel for. On the whole, however, it's a connection that's not about my illness. And this has broken a pattern of decades.

Kristin

Ten years ago I was the target of an intervention. Not about drinking, drugs, or insufferable behavior. It was about dating. Two friends set me up: invited me to breakfast, then told me I was going to go on eHarmony that weekend. No excuses. They were even going to give me a scholarship.

I had been dating, off and on, since my divorce several years earlier. Nothing lasting. But this seemed serious. eHarmony is one of those "find your lifemate" sites—not just a hook-up. The friends were persuasive. And they wanted a report after the weekend. So I signed up, completed the roughly 100-question compatibility questionnaire, poured myself a (generous) glass of cabernet, and started reviewing my matches.

Everybody who came up seemed nice. Some seemed reluctant; some felt desperate. Many had surprisingly cliched opening lines. And almost everyone looked suspiciously good for their ages. I guessed it was a mistake for me to include only recent photos. Actually, there's a story here—I hate getting my picture taken, and all I had was travel photos from a business trip to China: Garry on The Wall; Garry at Tiananmen Square. Garry in the Forbidden City.

I had nothing to report from the weekend. I left it alone until, distracted in a dull meeting Monday morning, I logged on. The first match that came up was

Kristin. "Hoping to make the world a better place…" was her intro line. Somehow it just sounded convincing to my jaded ears. The more I read, the more I liked this Kristin: fresh, forthcoming, unpretentious. Sincere. Oh, and she was beautiful.

I hesitated. But then I knew I was late in reporting progress to my friends. More important, though, I thought "if I'm going to be in this thing, I'm really going to be in this thing." I responded to the match, with little confidence that I would hear back. At the end of the two-hour meeting, I checked my phone. It was Kristin, responding! She asked me a few (thoughtful) questions, and if I lived in China (no! Baltimore).

We spoke by phone and she was charming—not in the "oh, this is me being charming" way, but in a forthright and thoughtful way. And she was a remarkable listener. She still remembers things I told her in those early calls.

Kristin was off to vacation on Cape Cod, and our electronic communication got spotty. She blamed it on a weak signal at her friend's cottage, and I thought—"oh yeah, the weak signal play." Yet it wasn't. She called me and said "I know it might sound like I'm losing interest, but I'm not. I do want to meet you." When she returned to her home in DC, we planned our first date.

The date was a three-hour affair, with many courses at the French bistro, and two bottles of wine. So much to talk about, so much common ground. And values.

Then, as things were winding down, Kristin said, "I know I don't want to get involved with someone who suffers from depression. I've just been through that, and

I went through that with my husband, too. It takes too much from me."

I had thought I disguised it well, but I was stunned. Did I somehow show that side of myself? I certainly didn't bring it up on a first date. Or was it just a cruel coincidence? I concluded that I just didn't know, and tried to file it away for later. I walked her to her car, asked if I could see her again (yes), and kissed her (kind of in the middle of the street). It was nice, so nice.

The next morning I reported to my matchmaker friend. Most of my report was about the depression topic that emerged at the end of our time together. His guidance: Full disclosure, now. His logic: If she's going to reject you for your depression, let it happen as soon as possible. It will hurt less. But there's a chance, admittedly small, that if you're honest about it, she will respect that and even feel some empathy. I crafted an email that morning in which I told Kristin the whole story of my depression, in reasonable detail. I noted that I take responsibility for it, don't blame those around me, and have the best treatment possible at Johns Hopkins, ongoing.

Kristin responded as my friend and I had hoped. We've been together ever since.

My depression was largely under control when I met Kristin—managed with lithium and nortriptyline, with weekly therapy. The excitement of getting to know Kristin brought me to a higher level of mood, blurring a low-level depression that seemed to never go away. I had almost come to accept it, yet was thrilled when new love eclipsed it.

Over time, months I'd say, the low-level depression gained momentum, and I was sensing some of the old advanced warning signals. Declining interest in favorite activities, and a barely perceptible sensation of slowing down. Kristin sensed it too, and communicated it to my psychiatrist at the time, Dr. A. The momentum built, and hospitalization looked more and more inevitable. In time, I was admitted.

Kristin was faithful: Visited every day, conferred with my doctors, and was as loving as ever towards me. The rest of this story is in Hospitalization #4. It would have been a completely different experience without Kristin's loving support, which she shared unreservedly even when I felt I didn't quite deserve it.

When Kristin responded to my email "confession" with empathy and respect, I knew I had met a very different kind of woman. The more I got to know her, the more I understood that she, too, had known hard times and profound disappointments. They were sources of empathy and understanding for her. And her way is to work from the premise that "we're all doing the best we can." Though never clinically depressed—at least not diagnosed—she is one of those rare people who really seem to understand what that medical condition entails, nonetheless.

It did not take me long to fall in love with Kristin. Her sharp intelligence is nearly matched by her sharp humor. What really "sold" me on her was when I saw the way her adult sons look at her. I've seen that look before, when my adult nieces look at Joyce, their mom. Deep appreciation, respect, love.

Kristin, now my wife, and I share an enviable life. Lots of joint interests. But mostly, talking. A continuous dialogue. That started on the phone from the Cape. And our latest topic is especially exciting: our first grandchild.

I'd honestly assess that Kristin is my perfect mate. Would I change anything? Just her tendency to generate solutions to my problems when what I'm actually seeking is empathy. We're talking about that.

Kristin was there at the worst depression of my life. And now she is here at my point of greatest happiness. Which makes sense, because she is absolutely central to that.

Fear

" Let me go first," I said, when I asked one of my doctors about the chance that I would relapse into major depression. "I'd say 50 percent." That's optimistic, he observed, in full scientific mode. (I was actually overstating my estimate in hopes that he would present a reassuringly lower number.) "With a history like yours, the odds are not with you. We need to be realistic about that. At the same time, we will do everything we can to keep you healthy and out of the hospital."

The fear I felt in that moment was neither new nor unique. In fact, it's always there, like I imagine a cancer survivor's underlying vigilance might be. The gap between my current positive and optimistic mood and how I would define full mental health is the undercurrent of fear.

Nightmares are a regular feature of my sleep. Some have obvious sources, like replays of when I was beaten at age fourteen by a gang. Some are classic anxiety dreams. But many are directly, or indirectly, grounded in depression themes. Hospitalization; ECT; crying spells. Others, however, are more subtle: struggling to concentrate; slowing down; underperforming.

The paradox: the better I feel—that is, the less depressed I feel—the more unsettling the fear of another major depression. I think it's a simple equation: I have so much more to lose. Of course, it could be deeper than that. And there is a deeper paradox—when I'm depressed I'm not fearing that it's going to happen. It already has.

Few things distract me from this fear. A couple of glasses of wine diminish it, yet more than that will exacerbate it. Being out on the water, especially if I'm piloting the boat. That is so fully engaging that fear does not have room to reveal itself. The healthiest and most reliable is being with Kristin; she has the effect of calming and centering me like nothing else. Even right after one of *those* nightmares.

I've concluded that the fear is here to stay. And it may be, in some ways, functional and adaptive. It certainly reminds me to do all the things I know I must do to stay healthy. Regular and adequate sleep; good nutrition; regular exercise; periodically checking my Beck Depression Inventory (BDI); and seeing my psychiatrist every one to two weeks. Of course, taking my various meds religiously.

It may further serve as an "early warning system," letting me sense when things seem to be sliding. Indeed, it operated in this capacity just recently, after we made a minor adjustment to my meds. I contacted my psychiatrist, and we decided to undo the adjustment. I seem to be reverting back to where I was. The early warning system did its job.

I am fortunate that I have the additional advantage of a psych-savvy spouse, who sometimes detects slippage before I do. I suspect she has a similar, but external, warning system. Together we have direct conversations, comparing perceived symptoms, and sometimes approach the psychiatrist as a solution-seeking team.

Hospital, Part 4

I can only remember three things that took me to my fourth hospitalization. First, the process of slowing down proceeded with alarming speed. Second, I asked for fifteen minutes of my boss's time to explain that I would be out for a while. Third, I had to tell my fiancé, Kristin, that one of those deep depressions I had confessed to her was underway.

I was never so depressed in my life.

Between hospitalizations at Hopkins, I was treated by a series of resident psychiatrists. Each one was terrific in her or his individual way, a mental health luxury of sorts. Generally, we would meet weekly for an hour, focusing on mood checks, problem solving, and reinforcing solid mental health habits. The medical regimen stayed surprisingly consistent: lithium and nortriptyline. With the occasional "kicker" (an anti-psychotic such as aripiprazole).

This combination of talk therapy and meds kept me, more or less, within the 80 percent well, 80 percent of the time goalposts. I wasn't feeling as good as I knew I could (especially when compared to the phenelzine days), but my Beck scores and daily routines were reasonable—and I knew significant happiness whenever I was with Kristin.

But as I had experienced in the past, what worked well for a long stretch, started to fail me. The propping up that I felt on the drug combination weakened, and threatened to collapse. And it did.

I have no memory of going to the hospital, how long I was there, or much of what happened. My resident psychiatrist, Dr. A., treated me with compassion and unrelenting encouragement (which was not my total experience with doctors during this "visit," as I'll explain later). I could tell that she could tell that I was in an immobilizing depression. Whereas in the past I was pretty much the model patient, this time I had none of the energy for that. It was her view—not surprising, considering my past responsiveness—that ECT was called for.

I don't know what was different this time, but after my second (I believe) treatment, I developed a powerful aversion to the process.

My aversion progressed into a full-blown phobia. I felt that one of the doctors had it in for me. This unhappy overlay was on top of the fact that I wasn't getting better—I wasn't responding as I had in my previous hospitalization. Every reasonable accommodation and more was made by the team: I would go first in the morning, go directly into the treatment room, my fiancée would come too until the propofol knocked me out. I even suspect they asked the doctor I feared not to be part of my treatment.

But I wasn't responding, at least not in a healthy way. After several treatments, I developed delirium. I wasn't sure where I was, why I was there, why these people wanted to hurt my brain, why the doctors didn't like me, and when it would all end—and how. The most dramatic chapter in my delirium is when Kristin, visiting, asked me, "Do you know who I am?" I knew this was an important question, and I reached with all the concentration I could put together and tried, "You are Kristin?" Yes.

The next question was tougher: "Do you know our relationship?" Oh man, this seemed like a critical question. I didn't want to blow it. I hesitated, thought through a few options, and offered: "We are going to be married?" Yes. Answering these two questions exhausted me—I needed to sleep.

I slowly improved, my memory returning in fits and starts, and my depression was lifting, albeit at a tedious rate. And I was lobbying to be discharged. My primary psychiatrist remained dedicated, steadfast, and warm. At the same time, I felt some of the doctors saw me as a problem—an ECT resister. Can I be sure, no. Yet I had a more positive reception in my previous hospitalization when I had been the ECT poster child. Perhaps what I was feeling was just their professional frustration. But it certainly contributed to my desire to leave as soon as I could.

In time—not sure how much—the doctors relented and discharged me.

Complication: Kristin had been called to Minneapolis to help with her sister's surgery and recovery. I had to stay with a friend in Baltimore—ironically, someone who had been in the Hopkins medical school administration years before. I remember nothing of that visit, other than being deeply afraid of the family dog (probably a Lab). The "slowing process" was well underway in a day or so, and it seemed I was experiencing every psychiatric reaction except hallucinating. I am not sure if this wasn't happening as well. My friend took me back to Hopkins.

I felt defeated, hopeless.

Gradually, through whatever combination of means, I emerged from the immobilizing depression. Gradually is the critical term here. Unlike my previous hospital-ization, where I fairly bounced back and set off for the London office in a matter of weeks, this time I missed an entire quarter of work. Even then, when I returned, I tired quickly, and had residual issues with concentration and "sharpness." Clear liabilities in my field, Finance.

I left the hospital with bupropion added to my lith-ium and nortriptyline. Also added was aripiprazole. They carried me for several years, until I decided I wanted more. My 80-80 goalposts seemed to be drifting away. And, besides, I wanted to find my way back to *better* ratios. Maybe even the levels I experienced 30 years earlier with an MAOI. I brought this vision to my new resident.

Post-Hospitalization
and into the World

From our initial interview, my new resident (number 7), had a different approach. Instead of the standard list of questions—he had already researched my history to a remarkable degree—he asked a few select questions about goals. These seemed to be *the* questions for that time. As the Theosophists say, though it is often misattributed to the Buddha, "When the student is ready, the teacher arrives."

Resident number 7, Dr. F., liked making plans. And collaboratively, we developed a plan to move me from "doing okay" to thriving. In fact, as was his preference, it was a three-part plan based on contingencies.

I was heading into my most challenging season at work. And I was feeling a little shaky. Not really slowing down, yet, but slipping to a degree that was noticeable— and confirmed by the Beck Depression Inventory.

We decided that the longer-term goal was to move me into a higher level of health, reflective of the thriving that phenelzine had produced more than three decades before. But first, we needed to make it through the summer. We increased the frequency of our sessions to more than once per week. We occasionally included my wife, who is psych savvy, from a medical family, and strikingly insightful. Meditation was encouraged—and practiced daily. Exercise stepped up. In short, we took on some time-tested techniques for managing milder depressions. The net effect was that I didn't get any worse, but did not improve, either.

Surviving the summer, I was ready to work Plan B. We would try to switch to tranylcypromine, an MAOI that generally caused fewer side effects than phenelzine—especially the excessive weight gain. The challenge was I would have to stop bupropion, for risk of serotonin syndrome. Dr. F.'s first thought was that I would need to be hospitalized to weather what could be a depressive reaction to leaving the bupropion. But we thought it through, and decided I could remove the bupropion gradually, without entering the hospital, but we would monitor and keep that option open. After a couple of weeks fully off the bupropion, I would start a low dose of tranylcypromine.

I can only imagine that getting approval for this plan took some intensive work on Dr. F.'s part. MAOIs are a decades-old medication, tracing back to the 1950s. And they developed something of a bad reputation when safer antidepressants, like the tricyclics, came along. Not only is there a rigorously restrictive diet that MAOI's require to prevent a possibly fatal hypertensive crisis, but there are also a number of cross-drug risks that contemporary doctors may not be well versed in.

But we did get approval to proceed. I came off the bupropion over the course of three weeks, sensing a slight drop in mood, and a bit of the "slowing" that presages a deeper depression. This was past my crunch period at work—which, incidentally, I completed in impressive form. So I could afford to coast a bit.

We increased the tranylcypromine gradually, 20 mg/day, 30 mg/day, up to 50 mg/day. But the transition was not smooth. One morning I was just feeling that something was awry. I checked my blood pressure, and it was 180/110! I drove to Patient First where they confirmed those scary numbers, and insisted I go to the nearest ER. Kristin arrived from work and drove me to Hopkins' ER. By then my BP had come down a bit. Dr. F. was alerted and joined us in the ER. He had already consulted with some more experienced doctors, and said he wasn't ready to give up yet. The tranylcypromine was showing too much promise. He reduced the dose and told me to keep a log of my BP, paying close attention to the 30-minute period after taking the pills.

Dr. F. located a retired, world-renowned expert physician on MAOIs based in New Zealand who offered a solution. Take the doses throughout the day. That worked. No scary spikes in BP. We were able to work up to 70 mg/day as my spirit and sense of possibilities reemerged to levels I hadn't seen since my phenelzine experience.

As a welcome coda to the consult with the New Zealand doctor, he sent an updated, more liberal version of the diet restrictions. I followed them meticulously and had no issues with blood pressure from what I ate. I did continue to have mild spikes after my doses, and my internist added a calcium channel blocker which attenuated those to reasonable levels.

So where did this leave me? I'd say that tranylcypromine was approximately 80 percent as effective as phenelzine. But some doctors have worried that the phenelzine was *too* effective. My excessive energy, limited need for sleep, and uncharacteristic optimism could indicate hypomania. I don't know, but none of these mark my tranylcypromine experience. It's more of a feeling of well-being, the ability to deeply enjoy the daily activities of my life, and reasonable optimism about the future—and my role in it.

I was then working with my eighth resident, Dr. O., and it was a different focus from my past experiences. More driven by life enhancements, along with managing the more-or-less standard stresses for someone my age who is a husband, father, consultant, and friend. I looked forward to these biweekly sessions as genuine growth opportunities—such was the unique blend of psychiatric skill, empathy, and imagination of Dr. O. But always, the backdrop remained keeping all the good mental health practices that I've acquired—through necessity—over a forty-year span. My life then was rich, beyond what I could have imagined through my decades of struggle.

Clouds Gather Again

This is the chapter I never expected to write. After two years of more-than-reasonable success with tranylcypromine, familiar feelings that I thought were gone forever reemerged. My outlook was becoming more pessimistic, my thoughts more focused on what could go wrong. And I was slowing down—not just my thoughts, but the way I spoke and even moved. At each point of this progression, I had a reasonable explanation. I was putting in too many hours at work; I was feeling estranged from my children; my sleep patterns were interrupted. At first I believed my self-explanations. They felt reasonable. But as the sensations intensified, I had to work to maintain the belief that I was not becoming depressed. And I knew it.

Kristin challenged my explanations, which reinforced my reflex to support them. My resident psychiatrist—now number 8—raised the possibility that I was sliding into depression. That word—depression—was the scariest thing in my world. I cited evidence to challenge his view, but as I was doing that, I felt somehow dishonest. Dishonest to the doctor, and with the dreadful feeling that I was being dishonest with myself. At the doctor's suggestion, I gave myself a Beck Depression Inventory. The result was unambiguous: my score was in the Moderate Depression zone. I sought to confirm or disconfirm that diagnosis with my "Beatles test." I put on the second side of *Abbey Road*. No response—it didn't delight or depress me. Evidence that my depression was real.

It was now summer, and my busiest time at work (intern season). Also, my most critical time, as the success of these high-powered MBA interns is a key part of my end-of-year evaluation (and bonus). I was struggling to keep up as my ability to concentrate was diminishing week-by-week. What I lacked in concentration I tried to replace with repetition. I would read interns' draft reports twice at first, then three times. As my concentration (and memory) declined beyond the point where repetition would compensate, I simply stopped reading the reports. At that point I knew I needed to talk to my boss. There would soon be no hiding my condition.

I approached my boss with, it turns out, unnecessary anxiety. I reminded him of my mental health history, announced that I was again becoming depressed, and asked for a couple of weeks off to address my issue. He was great: "take as much time as you need," was his attitude. I honestly believed at that point that I could recover to at least a reasonable degree by removing the daily pressure of work. Seemed reasonable at the time, but being away from work for that period seemed to accelerate my descent. My days were now filled with rumination and—as a new element—guilt. I tried the Beatle test again, and the result was not good. I could not stand to listen to side two of *Abbey Road*—"anti-hedonia" had slipped into my mental state.

Dr O. tried a new antidepressant and again added an anti-psychotic (aripiprazole). I was not optimistic. Past experience told me that when the slowing down reached the point where I had to concentrate to speak several sentences in succession, the momentum of depression was against me. Nonetheless, I tried the new medicine regime. It did nothing to slow the descent.

After a couple of weeks, during which I became increasingly hopeless about everything, the doctor and I accepted the inevitability of hospitalization. While I typically resist the hospital as my depression builds, I had now reached the point where it was a welcome prospect. I felt that I could go no lower in mood or outlook, and started to fear for my safety. Not that I would consciously make an effort to end my life. But I felt as though a subconscious desire could put me at risk. At least in the hospital I would be protected from myself.

It took about a week for a bed to be available, and during that wait I wanted nothing more than to be admitted. When the day finally came, I was ready. In the past, the inevitability of hospitalization would somehow lighten my mood, sometimes to the point where I would question if I really needed to take that step. Not this time. My sense of relief, while real, was superficial and diluted by the darkness of my mood.

When I arrived at the hospital, its familiar prohibitions were actually comforting. No belts, drawstrings, shoelaces—even dental floss! My room had been engineered to prevent suicide by hanging. Even doorknobs were designed to slope downward, providing no point to attach a cord smuggled in. While I had no plan to harm myself, knowing that it was impossible was reassuring.

I had forgotten from my last two stays at this hospital that I would not be treated by my regular psychiatrist. It was a relief to know that I would be overseen by two veteran doctors whom I had remembered from both earlier hospital stays, and my occasional "service rounds" interviews where my case was presented to psych residents.

I was on a different unit this time, which was split between adult cases—mostly depression—and adolescents—most with eating disorders. This made for a somehow brighter population, and I appreciated how many of the younger patients had decorated their rooms, almost dorm style. Outside of sessions there was limited interaction between the two generations. This was especially true at mealtimes, when nurses and nurses' aides would sit across from each eating disorder patient and record their consumption.

For the most part, the nurses viewed me as a pro—someone who had been there before, knew the ropes, and was unlikely to cause trouble. There was an upside and a downside to this: they wanted me to be in their sessions (cognitive therapy, group, nutrition) as I elevated them through my experience and willingness to contribute. The downside was I had done all of these sessions multiple times before in my previous hospitalizations. I felt like I could have taught them, and in some cases done a better job.

Dr. O. had informed the attendings of my absolute aversion to the ECT option. I was not quite as certain now. I thought back to my first experience with ECT, and how briskly it moved me from absolute hopelessness to a sense that my life was not over. I would have done anything to repeat that effect, even that which I most feared, given my frightening bout with delirium during my most recent treatments. The doctors raised the possibility of ECT with clear reluctance. I responded, "Let's do it."

It was the first week of my hospitalization that I was prepped for ECT. That process was familiar. Not familiar was the new ECT suite. Whereas the one I was familiar with was small, cramped, and filled with dials, meters, and other gizmos reminiscent of Dr. Frankenstein's laboratory, this new one was almost stylish. Sleek and modern, with the scary equipment tastefully accommodated in veneered shelving in the actual treatment room. The vibe changed fundamentally—it was almost a pleasant place to be.

Going through the standard prep procedures was rote to me. IV fluids in the evening and overnight to counter dehydration and to produce a "better seizure." Nothing by mouth after 10 pm—not even water. Sleeping with the tube running out of my arm was a touch awkward. But the biggest hassle was remembering the IV pole when getting up to use the bathroom. In the past I had forgotten that and accidentally yanked the IV from my forearm. But this time I was vigilant—it was my first step in fighting my fear and getting back to the ECT suite.

I was wheeled to the suite at exactly 9 am. This was reassuring, and I didn't think I'd have much of a wait. Inside, there were eight beds, separated by curtains. They put me in bed No. 1! Good news, I thought. But the numbers had no ordinal value. I had to wait about an hour for my procedure, and I got more and more anxious. My blood pressure, viewable on the tv monitor over my bed, rose precipitously. The last reading I remember was 185/100. They consulted with the anesthesiologist, and gave me something to bring it down. It worked somewhat, but did nothing for my anxiety (to my disappointment).

In time, the physician who would do the procedure came to my stall #1. I believe he was alerted to my anxiousness, and he spoke in reassuring tones about what was to take place in the procedure room. It wasn't helpful as I had heard the spiel before, many times. I was about to say "forget it" when I felt my bed moving, rolling toward the procedure room.

I had the sense that everyone in the room—the doctor, the resident, the anesthesiologist, her assistant, and a nurse—had been alerted to my fear. Each greeted me and told me her or his role. They gave me oxygen, which smelled like plastic. Then the injection of the propofol. I started to say "no," but I was out before I could form the words.

I woke up back in stall #1 and was quite confused. I somehow thought the procedure didn't happen (did I stop them in time?). But by this time they were giving me the standard questions to test for confusion ("Do elephants fly?"). I realized I must have had a treatment, and I was feeling confused yet relieved.

After about thirty minutes of observation they wheeled me back to the unit, where a cold breakfast of scrambled eggs and toast was waiting for me. As I ate (I was hungry) I noted that I didn't have the usual headache that followed ECT. Twenty-four hours later I sensed my mood had improved. During rounds my doctor agreed. The treatment had worked, and worked very well.

It would be two weeks and six more treatments until the doctors were satisfied that the positive effect on my mood would hold. After twenty-three days they released me, with the agreement that I would do three to four additional treatments as an outpatient.

My experience of the typical three-week hospital stay suggests, at least for me, there is a pattern. In week one, I was relieved and grateful. The daily frustrations of a locked ward with everything remotely injurious removed are merely background noise. You are safe. The staff are focused on helping you. And the hard waiting is over. After a few days you take your first shower in the suicide-proof stall, and put on fresh clothes. The worst is behind you.

That brings the second week. At this point you realize you won't be here forever, and your awareness of the outside world rises. Frustrations build: not being able to go outside for fresh air; being under constant observation (even while sleeping); wanting to have a conversation with someone who is not suffering as you are. (This hospitalization was during Covid 19, and no visitors were allowed.) You are trying to build a mental map that includes both the hospital and the world beyond. And you feel not fully a part of either.

By the third week you just want to go. Your mood has recovered enough that you can imagine operating reasonably well in the outside world (something unimaginable just two weeks ago). You do your very best to demonstrate your mental health to the staff—especially the doctors on rounds. Your sense of time sharpens when it had been a blur. And you start negotiating your discharge date. This is the longest week, and the toughest one. A bit of a paradox as your mood is significantly better, but the frustrations with locked-ward living hit a crescendo.

On day 23 I was released with the agreement to start outpatient ECT the following week. Medications were lithium and nortriptyline, a combination I had taken post-ECT twice before. Kristin took me for the treatment and was able to stay with me the whole time, except for the procedure itself. That made it much easier, and her reassuring touch actually helped me keep the blood pressure down to a reasonable level. It was real progress against my near-phobia of ECT.

I was not able to continue this positive momentum, however. What started as seeming indigestion turned dramatically sharper. Having been hit by a car (mine), I knew serious pain. But this was worse. A trip to the ER, and several scans later, I was diagnosed with gallstones, an inflamed gallbladder, and pancreatitis. I was admitted to the hospital, and monitored for several days in hopes that the inflammation in those two organs would abate enough to make gallbladder surgery possible.

After three days, opportunity arose. I had my gallbladder removed the morning of day four and was discharged after day five. Good news and a remarkable relief of pain symptoms. But ECT was not recommended during my recovery, and that made me nervous. (Before my recent, more positive treatments, I would have been grateful for this prohibition.)

My mood, however, continued to lighten. The meds and the ECT had done their job.

As a footnote, lithium, my steadfast friend as an augmentation of my antidepressants, had outlived its usefulness. I had developed a noticeable hand tremor, took propranolol to manage that (somewhat), and needed tadalafil to manage the sexual side effects of the propranolol. We brought the lithium level down slowly, with no ill effects or depressive symptoms, and finally eliminated it. I lost ten pounds briskly and effortlessly. I do still take the aripiprazole, and that may be the next challenge. But for now, my inclination is not to tamper with unimagined success.

Parting Thoughts

As I write these concluding lines, I am sixty-seven years old. My overriding relationship to life itself is one of gratitude. It's hard not to look back with regret—regret for all the years of suffering and searching. But grateful, still, that the years have brought me to this place of relative peace, and frequent joy. Would that I had learned the truth of my condition, the ways to manage it, and found the highest-level medical intervention earlier in life. But I did in time, and I remind myself daily to look ahead. Look ahead with hope.

I have found "pools of richness" that were inaccessible to me in my depressed years. I often awaken in the morning with a song in my head. And when that fails, I reach for a CD. I have returned to playing the guitar after my 1976 Martin sat in the closet for decades, and my psychiatrist is encouraging me to join a musical group. I am most alive, however, when boating on the Severn River outside Annapolis. A level of tranquility I could not have imagined in my earlier days.

Most rewarding, however, is my second marriage—to Kristin—a relationship improbably arranged by an online dating service. We've been together for ten harmonious years. In that time I have been hospitalized twice, but Kristin was steadfast. Ours is a relationship tested by depression, but that lives beyond the darkness that consumed earlier connections.

My work life is full and rich—when I am well, which is most of the time now. I have decided to work for a few more years in financial communications before I retire, not because I must, but because I want to. The company has been fully supportive through my difficulties and recoveries over the last twenty years. The work is rewarding and I am good at it. And I have a number of genuine friendships among my colleagues.

As a patient, I have been seen and treated for half a century in some of the sketchier precincts of our national health care system, as well as in some of the good and great ones, including the world-renowned Johns Hopkins Hospital. Through a series of sickening psychic plunges so extreme that some are lost to my memory, I have persisted, and my gifted doctors have helped to keep me going. So have the remarkable nurses whose intelligence and compassion give a human touch to the often sterile technologies of modern medicine. In Hopkins I have found a "psychiatric home," and that is a source of profound confidence as I move through this phase of my life.

I have learned to monitor myself. I have developed and honed my own early warning system. Kristin serves as a second pair of eyes and ears. I pray that my disease is now in permanent remission. I hope I never again feel that slow decline that augurs another crash. But if it does, I know who to call. I know what to do.

Somehow, through all the dark times, I have persisted. So much struggling, but so much life has followed my near-death experience on that snowy bridge nearly five decades ago. I must have had some underlying faith that I could find my way to a better place. And I have.

Afterword

TEN THINGS I'VE LEARNED ABOUT MY DEPRESSIONS

1. Perfectionism, which I learned in hopes of compensating for my depressions, is not a treatment. It actually fuels depression.

2. Some meds don't work for me, some do. But none does forever.

3. Trusting yourself and your gut are good tools for staying out of depression, but not reliable or helpful when you're depressed. A paradox.

4. I always optimistically mis-ascribe depressive symptoms to something else when I'm sinking into depression.

5. When heading into depression I need to trust my wife and doctors more than trusting myself. Depression is a world of distortions.

6. Cognitive-based therapies are effective in the early stages of depression, but ineffective, and ultimately counter-therapeutic, in later stages.

7. So far, nothing works as quickly or as effectively as ECT—for me.

8. Perfectionism, again, is the enemy of recovery.

9. Recovery is a long, step-by-step process. It takes longer to recover from depression than it does to become depressed.

10. But recovery always comes. Even when I'm certain it won't.

About the Author

G arry Cosnett is a communication expert with broad experience. From videotape editing, to college teaching, to coaching a client for a network TV segment, to advising CEOs on critical communiques, he has helped others communicate impactfully for over 30 years. Currently Senior Advisor, Investment Communication for a major investment firm, he holds an MA in Communication Studies from the University of Iowa. An avid boater, he and wife Kristin are frequently found on the Chesapeake Bay in their runabout, *Erin Anne*.

This is his first book.